D1711876

P.46

Logosynthesis:
Enjoying Life More Fully

Recharge. Revitalize. Reconnect.

CATHY CASWELL

BALBOA.
PRESS
A DIVISION OF HAY HOUSE

Balboa Press books may be ordered through booksellers or by contacting:

Balboa Press
A Division of Hay House
1663 Liberty Drive
Bloomington, IN 47403
www.balboapress.com
1 (877) 407-4847

Print information available on the last page.

ISBN: 978-1-5043-8939-6 (sc)
ISBN: 978-1-5043-8941-9 (hc)
ISBN: 978-1-5043-8940-2 (e)

Library of Congress Control Number: 2017915288

Balboa Press rev. date: 10/11/2017

Disclaimer

The content is the author's personal perspective and is provided only as general information. The material is not meant to be a substitute for medical treatment nor a promise to solve problems. The author accepts no responsibility or liability for misuse of the information contained in this book.

Logosynthesis is a registered trademark and used with permission of Dr. Willem Lammers.

No part of this publication may be reproduced in whole or in part; stored in a retrieval system; or transmitted in any form or by any means, electronic, mechanical, photocopying, recording, or otherwise without written permission of the publisher. Any requests for photocopying, recording, taping, or information storage and retrieval systems of any part of this book should be directed to:

Cathy Caswell, 1500 Waverley Rd, Waverley, Nova Scotia B2R 1W7.

Contents

Foreword

We are life energy, and this life energy is either flowing freely or frozen in patterns.

When our energy is in flow, we feel alive. We live from love, and we work from meaning. There is an awareness of what is good for us and what is good for those around us. We know what we want, and we're willing to go through the fire for it. We know what love is, and nothing keeps us from loving.

When our life energy is frozen in patterns, it doesn't flow. It's bound in body symptoms, in mental states, in relationships, in circumstances, and in an environment that doesn't change. The core characteristic of a pattern is its repetitiveness. It's the same each day, each week, and over years. The workplace is dull; the people are boring; and the days pass without fun, without joy, without meaning, and without growth.

Our lives seem like blind mirrors of what once kept us alive and vibrant. The cocoons that once protected us have become cages for so long that we can't imagine we have ever flown.

Cathy Caswell's book departs from a pattern of frozen energy, and it describes how she moved through it into a position of taking charge of her own life again, wriggling herself free from the burden that buried her.

Cathy's story is quite normal. You grow up, you meet challenges, you overcome them, you're trained in a profession, you get a job, and you get married. You find a family, and it seems as though all the ingredients are there to live happily ever after.

However, life isn't a fairy tale. Those tales tell children how to grow up, meet a mate, and find a mission. The magic in fairy tales tells them that life can offer brilliant solutions to insurmountable problems. That way, children learn that there is no problem without a solution, and that's good. If we flooded our children with problems only adults can solve, they would die before they could start to live.

Once we've grown up and found our place in a new family and in a job on a team, we have to learn what responsibility is without someone taking care of us on a daily basis. Cathy learned to work hard as a child, but the limits to that work were set by a pair of hardworking, loving parents.

When she took a job, found her partner, David, and founded a family, nobody set limits anymore. On the contrary: In her large family of origin, Cathy was taught early to do things even before she was told. That made her responsible wherever work had to be done, despite health problems. It seemed to be her mission to be there for others—for all others in need.

All of her life energy was now frozen in patterns. Her days were determined to be filled with obligations from dawn until long after dusk.

The limits showed up slowly. In the beginning, they were denied and muted in more of the same. Later on, they became impossible to deny and took the form of shame, guilt, and sadness because she could no longer do what she saw as her task in the world.

Cathy's story is one of transformation. I've been a witness to this transformation, and I feel honored and grateful that I've been able to play a role in it through my development of Logosynthesis.

In a firsthand account, Cathy describes in this book how she started to recognize the patterns, memories, fantasies, and beliefs that limited her. She became aware of how these frozen patterns triggered her into frozen emotions: shame, guilt, anger, and despair.

She also discovered how a simple technique, which she learned to apply by herself, seemed to soften and slow the harshness and immediateness of the pattern. That way, she created little pockets of insight that made it possible to reflect on the pattern and learn to act differently. She also learned that she doesn't have to solve everything on her own and that she could count on my dear colleague, Trish North.

Through the persistent repetition of the Logosynthesis procedure, Cathy freed her own life energy from the hidden programs that had determined her thoughts, emotions, behaviors, and beliefs for such a long time.

With the help of the Logosynthesis sentences, she became able to use her brilliant, rational mind for what it's made for: to think about the world as it is—not as it could be, not as it should be, not as it could have been, not as it should have been. Only when we can think about the world as it is, without the bias of previous generations and with a clear awareness of our mission and the corresponding potential, can we solve problems in the present.

If you recognize your story in Cathy's book, Cathy's solutions may support you in finding your way to go through the fire to find who you really are for your mission in this life, without driving yourself into exhaustion, without alienating those near you, and with full access to your potential.

Willem Lammers
Founder and Developer of Logosynthesis
Maienfeld, Spring 2017

Preface

This is not a story of my life falling apart or of leaving town to find myself. It is not a tale of an exciting trip to discover my true passions. There is no drama about needing to escape my life and start over. No, this is a story about allowing my life's journey to unfold from inside rather than always drawing from people, places, things, or events on the outside.

Looking back five years, I was overwhelmed with the routine of work and family life. I was coping, and I didn't feel that I had to change. I believed I was doing the right things the right way. However, I felt constant pressure to do it all. I worked hard to control situations and make people do things the way I knew they should be done, but I could feel that my reactions to everyday life were not allowing me to be who I wanted to be. I wanted to let go, but my reactions repeatedly sabotaged me—the same behaviors every time, regardless of how deep the breath I took to fend them off. Over and over, I found myself saying, "I can't believe I just did it again!"

Given my tendency to overreact, I recognized that I owed it to others to make a change. I knew this would be no glamorous undertaking, and I had no idea of the possible results. It involved reading many books, attending personal development sessions, and spending time on self-reflection. For me, an inner drive to fix myself while maintaining all that was important to me turned into a fascinating journey to find peace, contentment, and success right where I am.

Through this process, I have recognized that I am blessed with everything anyone could possibly want. I have moved from a state of always wanting more to a state of being content with what I have and allowing life to unfold with all its wonder. That's not to say that I don't have challenges, get frustrated, or react to situations that don't suit me. I sometimes wonder if people even notice how I have changed because this work involves my energy and not my physical self. Comments from others suggest they do notice a lighter side of me. Regardless of what others see, I am convinced that I am in a much better spot now than I was a decade ago. I can sense a shift. I can now start to let go of my reactions and my need to control. I don't say, "I just did it again," quite as frequently.

As I sat typing away at the public gardens in Halifax one beautiful evening, I apologized to the person beside me for mumbling to myself. She expressed that she didn't notice, but that it appeared that I was really enjoying what I was doing. I hope to share my insatiable wonder on the topic to provide you with a curiosity to further explore Logosynthesis.

Introduction

We live in a busy world filled with authoritative voices telling us what to do and action plans telling us when and how it should be done. In an effort to alleviate tension, we search out more information to help us cope, which often adds to our level of stress. We sense that if only we could fix the people and the things that bother us, we would be able to relax and enjoy life more fully.

It took a slightly accidental encounter to allow me to more fully appreciate that not only was I reacting to past experiences, but that also I could let go of these reactions so that things no longer bothered me. My role was not to fix others or force them see my point of view, but to create space to appreciate the contrast in thoughts and build something greater. This book is a result of meeting a cousin, Dr. Willem Lammers, and being introduced to a unique philosophy and technique that he discovered. Logosynthesis is a simple and eloquent process that is derived from many schools of thinking, yet the principles are combined in an effective system. It recognizes that our Essence, or core self, does not suffer, but through experiences in our life, our energy becomes dissociated or frozen. Using the recognized power of words to shift energy, Logosynthesis guides us through a series of specific steps to reintegrate this energy. The process allows us to be less reactive to the triggers of our past experiences and create space for things that are important in our life.

I can rely on physical activity, healthy eating, proper sleep, yoga, and prayer to keep my body, mind, and spirit strong and balanced. With Logosynthesis, I have been able to recognize the power of my spirit (energy) to neutralize my reactions. I have become more aware of how my actions are fueled by emotional, energetic reactions to past events. Above all, I have been able to identify the triggers and neutralize these powerful and often inappropriate reactions.

When I first started using the technique, I thought it was an easy tool that would allow me to break all my bad habits. I have discovered that knowing the technique is not enough. The most significant hurdle was to recognize that I held a great deal of energy in my beliefs. As I learned to let go of this energy, I could begin to create space for better choices.

We can all benefit from neutralizing our reactions and letting go of the energy bound in our beliefs, memories, and fantasies so that we can cope better with life, embrace opportunities and challenges, and more fully enjoy life. This book is presented to provide background information to help explain the process and provide an overview of the technique. It will allow you begin to work on your own with tips to guide your personal work. You don't need to fully understand to begin. The key is to start now. This book is a resource to get you started and guide you along your journey.

I was initially attracted to Logosynthesis because I could explore it on my own. When I first learned the process, I did not have a deep understanding of the theory or techniques, but I had a starting point that I could work from right away. I liked that the technique worked quickly and was easy to learn and that I could self-coach. I had the ability to choose what I wanted to work on when it suited my schedule.

I could begin on my own. Gradually, I reached out to coaches and certified practitioners for additional help, and I noticed enhanced results. Today, I both work on my own and within the Logosynthesis community—and my intrigue continues to grow.

In addition to personal development, there is great potential of Logosynthesis for broader health and wellness initiatives. As a society, we often talk about mental health, but as individuals, we are reluctant to reach out for help for fear of being labeled. If we can manage our stress within the norms of society, we are considered normal, and there is no need to do anything except maybe lose a few pounds, eat a little healthier, or fit in an extra workout. If we admit we need some help, we are labeled and pulled into the system. I believe that we are all somewhere on the same spectrum. Life happens to all of us. From the lazy and the lonely to the active and the achievers, we all react to life's unique events based on the triggers and beliefs that we have formed over a lifetime. We can all use some help to let go of the energy bound in the descriptions that society uses to define us. We all have room for better choices.

Logosynthesis is a unique system that has been developed in a tightly controlled group of experienced practitioners to help clients deal with trauma and anxiety. The work is powerful. It has been developed from a foundation in ancient knowledge, psychotherapy, energy psychology, and spirituality. The process has been fine-tuned over ten years of practice. Those who have been involved with it from the beginning appear to be hooked. Not only are my personal results compelling for me, but also those experienced through shared learning.

This book is written to share my experiences and learning so that you can apply Logosynthesis as a personal development and wellness tool. This is not meant to replace, but rather to supplement healthy lifestyle initiatives. Through my experience and education, I have come to recognize that spirit has a significant impact on wellness. Logosynthesis is a tool that guides us to get in touch with our spirit, or Essence, and uses the power of words to restore our flow of life energy. With practice, this simple technique becomes a powerful self-coaching tool to rise above our limiting beliefs, our painful memories, and our fantasies about a perfect life. I feel the technique and philosophy truly deserves to be shared with the world for the good of humanity.

In discussing the topic with friends and colleagues, I am aware that people struggle to understand it. I have come to realize that everyone has to reach a level of personal acceptance at their own pace and through their own means. The beauty is that you don't have to understand the process for the work to be effective. Simply following the process outlined can deliver powerful results.

The goal of this book is to help you begin to help yourself to create more enjoyment in your life rather than waiting for others to fix the things that bother you. It is written to raise awareness, to initiate conversations, and to create excitement around the ability to support individuals and groups using the power of words with a unique and powerful technique—Logosynthesis.

Chapter 1: Can We Enjoy Life More Fully?

Our beliefs convince us that we are doing okay and have things under control. We all may be doing fine, but we have an opportunity to do better.

We Think We Are Fine

Why should I care so passionately about letting go of my reactions and my need to control? I'm fine. Really. I have an amazing and beautiful family. I have a great home in a wonderful community and a good job with lots of benefits. I am healthy, happy, and content. I don't generally worry about the future or dwell on my past. There is some stress in my life, but it's nothing I can't manage. I am busy living a very good life.

So how do I know that I have work to do?

When I listen to the repeated chatter in my mind, I can hear it. "Hurry up, and get it done. Do a little more. Don't waste time watching TV. Don't let your team down."

When I sit quietly, I can sense it. Tight shoulders. A pit in my stomach. A clenched jaw. A stiffness in my chest.

When I go through my routines at home, I can feel it. Stress because I have too many things to do and not enough time. My mind racing. Tension in my voice. I am distracted and always in a rush.

When I press through my workday, I notice my reactions. The feeling of pressure to meet a deadline. The frustration when people aren't doing what they should be doing. An irrational angst about picking up the phone.

Most importantly, when I interact with my family, I know I still have work to do. The floor isn't swept the right way. The dishes aren't washed fast enough. The television is kept on during the day. I react.

I know I am not alone. Among family, friends, and coworkers, I notice similar themes, even if no one wants to admit it.

There is, for example, that group of stressed-out moms, the group who could easily be called the *perfect* moms. They have great families, the best parties, the nicest houses, and the most friends. Their efforts to maintain perfect homes and families require a lot of energy. They feel pressure to do it all—and very well. Their children have to be in a multitude of activities to make them well rounded and introduce them to the right group of friends. The house has to be clean, the meals healthy, and the laundry always done. These moms feel that they need to create fun family memories for their children to cherish, which normally involve special trips and parties. If you ask members of this group how they are doing, they say they are okay. Underneath, you can sense they are tired and stressed, but they know they have it all, so they say they are fine. Really.

There is another group of individuals who I sense are struggling to hang on. But still, when asked, they are quick to respond, "I'm fine. Really." They are reluctant to admit that life isn't manifesting as planned. Maybe they've experienced a traumatic event or a series of things have gone awry. Maybe they are not doing the work they dreamed of. Maybe their family situations aren't what they wanted. People in this group often have everything worked out in their minds, but other people get in the way, and events happen that they cannot control. They could use some help, support, and understanding, but everyone is busy, including them.

I notice children may appear to be fine, but they also react. A scolding parent, a scary movie, and a bully in the playground all elicit visible stress reactions in children. They may want others to believe they are okay. They may act tough, but if you watch, you can tell by their voice, their posture, and their actions that they could use some help.

For me, the most interesting group is made of individuals who adamantly believe they are doing just fine. Really. And by all accounts, they are doing great. They express interest in stress management—for their spouses, friends, or coworkers, of course. They watch the news, and everyone else is clearly messed up, but they are fine. They do not feel stressed. Their lives are comfortable, yet they have strong opinions on how the world should be and how people should behave. Things are black and white, right or wrong. Many in this group are in positions of control. They head up households, corporations, and organizations. They are in enviable positions to exert control over their environments and change things that make them uncomfortable. In their views, if others are feeling stressed, then it is others who need to change. Often, these are the individuals causing others to stress.

I guess we are all fine.

Really?

Don't be fooled. We can all do better. We convince ourselves that we are fine. We hold strong beliefs about the way life should be, and we work hard to maintain those beliefs, even when they cause stress to ourselves and others. Where do those beliefs come from? How can we uncover them and better manage our stress?

Our Beliefs Can Deceive Us

Life is full of experiences and events that form our beliefs. Our beliefs are powerful and operate in our subconscious thought patterns. We may believe we think rationally. In order to pay my bills, I need to keep my job even though I hate it. But think again; maybe you could buy less and have fewer bills. Maybe a better job is available. Your belief may be fueled by a personal experience, such as a parent who stayed in a job only to support the family. Beliefs drive our behaviors, and beliefs don't heed rational thought.

We form our beliefs beginning at a very young age. Of course, as infants and youths, we are not always in control of our lives. Highly emotional events that occur at a time when our brains are responsive to outside stimuli create beliefs that form our subconscious thinking and trigger our reactions much later in life. We will not likely be aware of this influence.

It is generally understood that beliefs are formed by a combination of thought and emotion associated with our experiences. During emotional events, good or bad, we release stress hormones to enhance memory. We also know that our beliefs drive the subconscious thinking that allows us to make split-second decisions to save our lives—fight or flight. Beliefs also drive the thinking that causes us to judge individuals before our conscious thoughts can weigh in.

Beliefs are responsible for the habits and routines that make our lives comfortable. Our subconscious thoughts drive our ideas of who we are and who we want to associate with, thus forming our unique personalities and characters. It allows us to make sense of all the chaos in the world within a manageable construct of how life should be. As long as things fit nicely in this box, we're okay.

But beliefs also create stress. We create fantasies about what our lives should be like. When everyday events do not match these fantasies, our bodies react with a stress response. We may not consciously think we are reacting, but our bodies have kicked into defensive mode.

The reality is that we cannot change others, nor can we change all the circumstances of our lives. All we have to do is change our beliefs! Easy enough? Perhaps—until we recognize a couple of things. First, beliefs tell us we are right, so it becomes difficult to rationally understand why we would change something we know to be right. Second, as I will explain throughout this book, beliefs are energetic structures residing in our personal spaces. They are formed by freezing energy as we experience life and when thought and emotion collide. Depending on the intensity of the experience, it can create powerful images or other sensory perceptions that stay with us. When a person or event challenges these beliefs, the reaction is outside of our rational thought process. We often think of it as a gut reaction. Because our experiences are unique to us, we may not fully understand our own reactions, nor do we understand the reactions of others.

We React to Our Environment

Stress and anxiety are associated, and the terms are often used interchangeably. Stress is the body's response to a situation and is classified as acute or chronic. Acute stress allows us to kick into survival mode without stopping to think about what we need to do. Chronic stress, often related to everyday life pressures, causes stress hormones (epinephrine and cortisol) to be released over a longer period of time. This can lead to serious health problems for us and—like secondhand smoke—for those around us (see Mate's *When the Body Says No: The Hidden Cost of Stress*).

Stress has been defined as a nonspecific response of the body to any demand for change. Nonspecific. Demand for change. Think about this definition. When an external event occurs that does not match your belief structure, it demands your body to change. Your body reacts with a stress response. You might take a deep breath and tell yourself to remain calm and that all will be well. But your body still reacts with a stress response. Sometimes, the response percolates below the surface. Other times, it might explode, exhibiting less than desirable behavior.

If we accept that our beliefs are generally formed at a very young age and often held outside of our conscious awareness, we can begin to understand that our bodies are constantly reacting to situations that arise in our lives. We think we are in control of our environments, and to make ourselves feel comfortable, we seek out situations that match our belief structures. Yet, we are constantly exposed to stimuli that do not match our beliefs. Our bodies are constantly demanded to change, and they consistently react with stress responses. We may not choose to be stressed. We may not even recognize or acknowledge stress. But we do have a choice in how we respond to stress. This can be explained as follows:

> Stress means "excess environmental demands on a person's resources." Everyone has different demands and different resources. We react by:
>
> 1. Changing the demands of the environment
> 2. Changing our resources
> 3. Changing the way we react to the environment
> 4. Doing nothing
>
> "Doing nothing" eventually breaks down. Changing the first three items can take a lot of energy. Logosynthesis allows you to change your reactions to the environment. As you react with more patience and wisdom, your resources may grow and you may be able to change that environment and the demands it puts on you. (Lammers, 2015)

We work hard to change the demands of our environment. The demands of my job stress me out; I'll find a new one. The demands of my family stress me out; I'll change our living arrangements. The cost of living stresses me out; I'll find a way to afford what I want. It takes a lot of energy to change it all.

We also work hard to change our resources. To get in physical shape, we sign up for expensive gym memberships. We rush across town during rush hour to attend a special class. We go out of our way to buy expensive food or supplements that have special nutritional properties. We have a long list of things to do to build our resources. In case we forget, the minute we turn on the television, a steady stream of messages reminds us. It is very easy to become so wrapped up in our beliefs about what we need to do in an effort to stay healthy that we unknowingly put excess demands on our body.

We could try to avoid situations. If we know that something stresses us out, we could simply stay away. I know that I am scared of heights, so I don't choose to spend a vacation biking in the mountains. Avoidance isn't always an option, however. Our need for a steady income, for instance, may compel us to work in a demanding environment.

We could make sure our body and mind are strong enough to manage this stress response. Through sufficient exercise, proper diet, and adequate sleep, we become better equipped to handle the stress when it occurs. We can even condition our brains to operate better when the stress response kicks in. Deep breathing is effective in helping us to think and find a pause before we react. We can be armed with lots of techniques to simply manage the stress response when it inevitably occurs.

We can avoid some stressors, and we can manage our reactions, yet the body will continue to react. There will always be a stressor of some kind. This response builds over time and affects us at levels, often beyond our awareness. Is there another way? Could we simply disarm the beliefs that lead to the stress? Maybe, but we first need to realize that our beliefs are unique to each of us and appreciate how deeply our beliefs are held.

Sensory Perceptions Trigger Reactions

Our emotional response to events in our life can be rated on a scale of mild agitation to moderate anxiety to severe trauma. Our biological stress response kicks in, triggering reflexes and releasing hormones, whether we acknowledge the response or not. With the heightened emotional response, sensory perceptions from the event become imprinted. Like beliefs, these emotional imprints are unique to each of us.

Think of a situation that has caused you to overreact. Why did you get so stressed out at the sound of someone's voice or at the sight of dishes in the sink? Why were you so afraid to speak in front of others or stay home alone? Why have you experienced these reactions repeatedly, despite your best attempts to convince yourself there is no need for concern? Whether it is a dry mouth, a pit in your stomach, a quivering voice, or a pounding headache, you know that your physical response is not congruent with the event that just occurred. You can't explain why you feel so strongly, but you can't deny your body's stress response. Friends and family may have difficulty empathizing because they can't see the underlying source of your stress—the imprints that trigger your reactions. They only see the effect: You are stressed. The recurrent nature of your response may lead others to tell you to just get over it and move on.

Because we don't fully understand and can't explain our stress responses, we may withdraw or use coping techniques. However, those won't change what the body experiences. Responses to triggers become engrained. We are born with a unique genetic code for a predetermined set of characteristics, but we are also born into a unique set of life experiences to which we respond. The circumstances that form belief structures and attitudes are not all within our control or within our genes.

I may want to avoid all negative events in my life and increase the intensity of pleasurable events. The reality, however, is that life happens beyond my conscious control. Life's events create my resilience and form my personality and character. Situations in my life cause stress and anxiety, and how I deal with them can impact my health, both short- and long-term. I may attempt to change my behavior through conscious effort and focus on my coping techniques, but my cognitive thought processes are not effective in disarming my emotional responses to these triggers.

Getting in touch with the energy and emotions that have created these deeply held imprints can be uncomfortable. For me, even sitting in silence was often distressing. We are trained to be cognitive individuals, thinking and analyzing our way to the right answer. But for me, this level of conscious thought did not allow access to the energy level necessary to identify and dissolve the triggers to my behavior. If a highly emotional event created the emotional imprint, it stands to reason that I needed to access the same thought and the same emotion in order to release that energy. Other people could not do this for me, nor could I do this for others. I needed to be willing to identify how I experienced stress and the sensory perceptions that triggered the response. I needed to quiet my space without jumping up to do the next thing on my list. I needed to feel safe to explore. And I needed a tool to guide me.

Raising Our Energy Awareness

Energy and spirit can be defined in many ways. According to the Merriam-Webster dictionary, energy is "a usually positive spiritual force," and spirit is "the force within a person that is believed to give the body life, energy and power."

Across cultures, energy is generally thought to be the source of life and has been given different names: Prana, Chi (Qi), or the Holy Ghost. In Logosynthesis, it is called Essence. Willem Lammers, founder of Logosynthesis, described it as follows:

> In Logosynthesis, the goal is to restore the flow of energy to allow for our true Self to be expressed. We acknowledge that we are composed of body, mind

and spirit. Our body is our physical matter, which can be compared to hardware. Our mind is our rational thought, which can be compared to software or programming. Our Essence, or spirit, is the energy that flows through the system to create.

Essence is the user of the body and mind and is felt when our systems are in flow, through meditation, sports, art, relationships. Our Self is Essence live, in time and space on earth. Our Self is a flexible, creative and dynamic system that wants to learn. Our Self is the starting point for our personal mission, to create meaning in our lives.

In the book *Power vs. Force: The Hidden Determinants of Behaviour* (David Hawkins, 1995), the author introduces the concept that our vibrational energy can be measured and that higher vibrations are associated with higher levels of human consciousness. The scale moves along a spectrum, with ratings for energy levels as follows: shame, 20; guilt, 30; apathy, 50; grief, 75; fear, 100; desire, 175; anger, 150; pride, 175; courage, 200; neutrality, 250; willingness, 310; acceptance, 350; reason, 400; love, 500; joy, 540; peace, 600; and enlightenment 700–1,000. Hawkins has observed that the lower energy levels are associated with force, always requiring something to move against. Force is driven by reactions and requires energy to produce results. Force polarizes and produces counterforce, resulting in win-lose relationships. In contrast, power, according to Hawkins, is generated from the higher vibrations and requires nothing from the outside. Power is still. It does not move, but influences everything around it, much like gravity. It is associated with compassion and noble principles. As we start to let go of the reactions tied to our beliefs, we can start to shift from exerting force in our lives to allowing our life energy to emanate power. For comparison, think of a boss who exerts authority through the use of forceful language and threatening statements. Compare that person to a boss who influences with encouragement and wisdom.

Even if we struggle to understand something we cannot readily see, as we increase our acceptance of the power of our energy and spirit, we will become more aware of how it manifests in our everyday lives. When we are disconnected, our stress becomes apparent through the urgent tasks that present. When we feel connected, things flow more smoothly, and we operate in a space that allows our creativity to flow. The challenge for each of us is to recognize the opportunity for better connection and to find a tool that is effective in shifting our energy to better connect us with our life purpose.

Chapter 2: A Journey to Neutralize Reactions

Like many people, I grew up okay. My unique set of experiences has shaped who I am today and influences the way I react to situations.

Forming Beliefs during Childhood

We all strive to be normal. We all work hard to cope and belong in our groups. If we are not normal and coping, life can become extremely challenging. I was blessed to grow up normal—not without challenges, but normal.

I will provide a personal overview, not to bore you with details of an ordinary life, but rather to provide perspective on how I got to where I am today. My childhood was not remarkable. However, like everyone, I experienced a unique set of life events that have left me with a unique set of beliefs, which drive my reactions today.

I grew up as the middle child in a large family on a busy dairy farm. My parents were Dutch Catholic immigrants who started with nothing and worked very hard to build the farm and family of their dreams. From my perspective, they were extremely successful. They instilled strong core values that have served my siblings and me very well over the years.

My early years set the stage for a great adulthood, despite suffering from undiagnosed celiac disease. My mother often said, "No one ever died from hard work," and despite not particularly enjoying hard work, I recognize it as an important ingredient to my success. But gradually, I started to notice that something was perhaps a little out of balance. While apparent to others, it took me a while to acknowledge that I was overly reactive. The challenge was despite knowing this, my reactions led me to focus on changing others and changing things to better suit me. I was fine.

Working Hard to Cope with Demands

In 2000, I was in my mid-thirties, and life was good. I was working in sales in a multinational food company with a dynamic group of coworkers. I enjoyed the fast-paced, stressful world of sales with sales targets and project deadlines. In addition to my career, I volunteered with a number of organizations. Most notably, I supported the Canadian Celiac Association toward its aims of education, advocacy, and awareness. Given the low awareness, this involved a great deal of work.

In 2001 and 2002, my husband and I were blessed with two beautiful, healthy daughters. Priorities shifted, and routines changed. We had great times entertaining family and friends, most with similarly young families. But life was starting to get very busy. I recognized that I had to look after myself: eat well, go to the gym or head out on the trail for a run, and get a good night's rest, despite late-night work events and children who required attention. I was running out of time and energy to get everything done.

By 2008, I felt like I was going to lose my mind. I had been working in the same role for four years. This was long for me as I had regularly changed positions throughout my career. I needed to think of my next career move, but many jobs were being shifted out of our region of Canada. This was one factor in creating nervous energy in the office, including the leadership team. The pressure to deliver sales results in a highly competitive market was felt by everyone. Some people quit. Others remained, but the environment was very intense. I realized that I had a choice. I could leave and pursue another job with my dietetics license and MBA, or I could stick it out and try to change things. I felt that as part of the team, I should stay and try to make changes.

My need to resolve this situation was heightened because of my family members. I really didn't want to drive them crazy, although I am sure they thought otherwise. I felt that the stress of work was influencing my behavior in my personal life. At this time, my husband was also faced with his role being moved out of the region. With careful consideration and good timing, we purchased a nearby community pharmacy. Our home on the lake had been recently renovated, and we loved to entertain family and friends from near and far on a regular basis. The girls were now going to school, so I wanted to get involved through the parent-teacher committee.

Not only was work busy, but I also managed to make my home life more than a little hectic. Heaven forbid that someone suggest that something had to give. Everything was important to me. I wanted it all, and I felt could do it all. If only I could control everyone to do things my way, at my pace and to my liking, life would be fine. However, deep down, I think I knew this plan wouldn't work so well. I think that as much as I believed that I was right, that others needed to change, and that I could do it all, deep down, I felt that I had some changes to make. But the specific problem was elusive. I couldn't quite grasp what to change and how to do it.

Recognizing Inappropriate Reactions

Over the next few years, I noticed I had no tolerance for things that weren't done right. Coworkers weren't working hard enough, my children weren't always doing what they were told, and my husband didn't always anticipate what I needed him to do. When I got together with friends, I found we were all experiencing similar situations, so it clearly wasn't my issue. They reinforced my belief that I was right.

Still, something did not sit well with me. I was convinced I was right. Yet, I sensed that maybe it was not only others who needed to change to please me, but that I had to change as well. The motivation to change myself persisted despite my friends reassuring me that I was fine. I trudged off to see a psychotherapist in an attempt to manage my reactions, but this just confirmed to me that I had to learn to cope with someone with a difficult personality. I read self-help books and

Logosynthesis: Enjoying Life More Fully

listened to audio books in search of the magic solution. To relax, I made time for massage therapy and the gym. I started getting up at five each morning to do a yoga routine. Recognizing that my energy wasn't great, I booked sessions with Healing Hands and Reiki. I was introduced to and intrigued by Angel Therapy. I had an insatiable desire to challenge my thinking and figure this all out. I made time for quiet, focused, happy thoughts, and I enjoyed laughter. But underneath, I was still reacting to the same things. People weren't doing what I believed they should be doing, and I was working on managing my reactions to that fact.

I had the perfect life, but I had a hard time keeping up and finding time to appreciate it. When I got stressed, I reacted. Many situations continued to drive me crazy regardless of how deeply I breathed or how long I paused. I continued to wonder why people weren't working harder, moving faster, or doing things the way they should be done. I continued to think that if people could just do things right, life would run so much more smoothly. I felt as though I sucked the fun out of everything for everyone. With all the effort I had exerted, I felt that I hadn't changed very much at all.

Listening to Self-Talk for Indicators

I recognized that my life was not perfect, but I had a very good life. I was living a normal life. My friends were facing similar frustrations as we progressed through the working parent phase of our lives. Here are a few of my reflections to illustrate the point. Do they sound familiar?

— I am normal.
— I have lots of friends who can verify that I am normal.
— I have everything that I could possibly want.

17

- My appearance is normal, almost a little too normal for my liking, but I'm lucky that I'm healthy.
- Well, I do admit that I should lose about twenty pounds.
- But at least I am normal.
- My personal issues are not things that I want to share with people.
- I have a few things that I would like to work through on my own.
- I don't want to talk about these things because it will probably just make things worse.
- I am busy with my to-do list, and I don't have time to dwell on what isn't working.
- No one wants to hear my problems, and no one would probably understand them.
- My feelings aren't that important anyway.
- I have no problem with putting things behind me and moving on.
- I do acknowledge that my energy isn't really good to be around.
- I hate the fact that my bad moods are so transparent.
- If people would just do things right and on time, I wouldn't be in a bad mood.
- I recognize that I am quick to zap the fun out of everything. I don't like that about myself.
- I know I have a lot of traits that are "just me." I can't seem to change these.
- I'm a lot like my mother. Family-focused. Results-oriented. Quick-tempered.
- I would like to change me, but all in, I'm in a great spot. I am very lucky.
- I feel as though I have the perfect life, but I just can't keep up to it all.

Creating Space for Spirit and Energy

Among the array of personal development books, I was intrigued by authors who told of experiences relating to the power of positive thinking. Many wonderful survival stories caused me to pause and ponder the power of spirit to override physical hardship. Stories of great achievement often attributed success to a spiritual force. For example, new-age spirituality authors, such as Ester and Jerry Hicks, drew on personal experience with spirit. Dr. Wayne Dyer shared passionate and inspirational teachings on his personal journey to wellness through spirit. Sarah Susanka explored the idea of a "not so big life" from her professional expertise as an architect. I discovered an interesting perspective in *The Law of Attraction: The Science of Attracting More of What You Want and Less of What You Don't* (Losier, 2010). Based on my results in trying the technique, I was intrigued.

I recognize that there is power in holding thoughts in your consciousness to manifest the desire—or in other words, make things happen. As I reflect on these synchronicities, I think that perhaps I don't use these techniques as often as I should, though I try to refresh it on an annual basis as things shift in my life.

Through this work, I had highlighted that I didn't want to feel a number of negative emotions that bothered me, such as being stressed, frustrated, and angry. I indicated my desire for characteristics such as calm, organized, productive, effective, and fun to be around. Everything I had learned to date, both personally and professionally, did not suggest that I would be able to make this change. I referred back to the energy work of David Hawkins. In a desire to feel better, I wanted to shift the lower, negative energies of fear, anger, and frustration to the higher, positive energies of acceptance, love, joy, and peace. However, I sensed there was a barrier to shifting my energy. In fact, I recalled a discouraging line in Hawkins's book, which indicated that human consciousness shifts an average of only five points over a lifetime. I declared to friends that I was working to be a kinder, gentler person. I was also working to make a positive difference at home, at work, and in the community. But based on my conditioning throughout my childhood, I did not want to give up my drive to be efficient and effective. I was still guided by a strong sense of what was right and just. I felt I could be as nice as the next person, but that I also had responsibilities to get a lot of things done right—and now. For me, this translated to, "People have to do things my way, on my timeline." Still, I did not understand, nor could I comprehend, how I could let go of this persistent thinking and still be effective.

Exploring a Unique Approach

I had a desire to become more calm, organized, effective, and fun to be around. I did not feel as though I was making progress, despite my heightened focus on a healthy lifestyle. I was heading to the gym, following a planned menu, and getting lots of sleep, but I was still stressed out. I did not respond well when people didn't do what I expected, both at work and at home. Because I was even busier trying to fit in all my healthy-lifestyle activities, I felt even more stressed and less tolerant when things did not go my way. I really had no comprehension as to how I could possibly change my stress levels to become a kinder, gentler person.

In 2013, through Facebook, one of my cousins in Ontario asked another of my cousins in Switzerland if he planned to meet me during his visit to Nova Scotia. Given my large family, it didn't surprise me that I didn't know Willem Lammers. I discovered that he came to Halifax annually to deliver workshops and training sessions on Logosynthesis. Of course, I had no idea what this was, so I looked it up online.

What I discovered intrigued me. The work was focused on trauma, but my mind translated the word *trauma* as *stress*. I read about Willem's idea that emotional events can freeze energy in our personal space by creating imprints. These energy structures trigger our reactions to events that happen today.

Perhaps this work could help me control my reactions. I was curious to learn more about the topic.

Although my life was busy and this work sounded a little out there, I was very curious. All my personal development work to date had opened my mind to such ideas, especially those around energy and subconscious thought. My professional background around the elusiveness of accessing emotions (energy) to change our behavior further intrigued me. This technique sounded so easy. I decided to free up some time to explore.

During Willem's visit to Nova Scotia later in 2013, he joined my brother, sister, and our families for a meal, and we talked about a number of common interests, mainly food, travel, and politics. We didn't discuss energy, psychology, or his work. It was simply a pleasant visit to learn more about each other and our families.

As I continued through my routines at work and home, however, I noticed many situations where I felt Logosynthesis might help. I was hesitant to suggest the process to others because I wasn't comfortable enough with the language. How could saying three sentences heal a relationship or provide relief for deep grief? I felt compelled to understand the topic better. I needed to work on it at my own pace. And I needed to find a way to talk about it in everyday terms.

Willem visited us again in 2014. It was much the same as the previous year: a lively discussion over a meal with family. But this time, as I drove him back to his hotel, I told Willem that I was intrigued by Logosynthesis and wanted to find a way to make it more mainstream.

I wanted to align this work with a healthy-living program I had been conceptualizing for my husband's pharmacy. Willem was receptive to the idea, but his work at the time was quite demanding: expanding practice groups internationally and developing new material for master classes. I knew that I could run with the idea, but I lacked time and expertise. From my work with the Celiac Association during its infancy, I understood that an important task was not only to start talking about the topic, but also to develop a language that resonated with people so that we could shape the conversation. From my new understanding of Logosynthesis, I understood that I had emotional imprints that were holding me back from even talking to others about it. A great deal of my work called for peace and quiet, so early mornings became my friend. My work began.

In the following chapters, I attempt to share this fascinating topic. I hope it will help you understand a new approach to healthy living, allow you to tap into the power of your spirit, and provide you with a tool to neutralize your reactions so you can better cope with the challenges of life and enjoy life more fully.

Chapter 3: Let's Talk Logosynthesis

Energy is in flow or it is frozen.

Energy is in the right or wrong space.

Words can move energy.

—Dr. Willem Lammers, 2015

The Discovery of Logosynthesis

Dr. Willem Lammers has engaged in a successful career of psychology, psychotherapy, coaching, workplace counseling, and guided change. On January 11, 2005, he was asked by a colleague to meet with a client who was unable to make further progress in her therapy. The client, Lenore, was a petite forty-two year-old woman who appeared to have deep fear and uncertainty. Her life had shifted dramatically in one day, five years earlier, when she had fallen down a set of stairs at the train station on her way to work. She could not recall the events around the fall, but she had found herself in an unfamiliar place hours afterward, bruised and with her clothes torn. After this incident, her whole life changed. She experienced anxiety, could no longer concentrate, and had to leave her job. She became fearful, uncertain, and unable to cope with life. She consulted doctors, but they found nothing neurologically wrong with her. Although Lenore and her husband were convinced that her difficulties started with the fall five years earlier, doctors and health insurance agencies denied it and diagnosed a personality disorder.

Willem's colleague believed that the symptoms were related to post traumatic stress from the event. Lenore was relieved to have acknowledgment of her condition, but the symptoms showed little change, and the amnesia remained. Willem was asked to consult based on his experience with energy psychology. He listened to Lenore explain that she felt disoriented and crazy; her Swiss-German dialect translated to "beside my shoes." She often reached for doors that were eight inches to the left of her body. Her words "beside my shoes" resonated, and he wondered if part of her life energy could have shifted because of the accident. He asked if she was ready to try an experiment. Lenore was curious and had nothing to lose, so she agreed.

Willem asked her to retrieve the energy from the body beside her and put it back into herself. She reacted with intense fear. After some reassurance, he made a second attempt. Lenore became highly agitated, and it was evident that something was shifting. He decided to wait. After about twenty minutes, she calmed. When he probed about the incident five years earlier, she was able to recall the event for the first time. She had been pushed down the stairs and was left lying on the ground, frozen in terror. When she found her car, she was unable to unlock the door. She tried to take the train home, but she couldn't open the automatic door, and the train left without her. She finally managed to contact her husband, and he took her home. Lenore was relieved to regain these memories. The split between her consciousness and her body had healed.

Willem concluded that the trauma of Lenore's fall had resulted in a degree of dissociation that had affected her ability to cope with everyday situations. He believed that if he could guide Lenore to locate the dissociated energy and return this energy to the right place within herself, he could do the same to help others.

Developing the Sentences for Logosynthesis

For Willem, the next few years involved further exploration and refinement of the technique. He coined the name *Logosynthesis* from two Greek words meaning *to put together with words*. It is based on ancient spiritual belief that words have a manifesting power beyond their content. This idea goes as far back as the origin of creation: Words have the power to activate energy. Based on the realization that words were able to shift energy, his task was now to determine which specific words to use to help other people. Through trial and the efforts of a core group of interested therapists, the words were put into sentences. Willem and his colleagues determined that three areas of energy were frozen in emotional imprints.

The first was energy that belonged to the person that was no longer available. It was frozen in the energy structure formed by the emotional event.

The second was energy that belonged to someone or something outside the individual but was frozen in their personal space.

The third component was energy that was bound in the individual's reaction to the event.

A set of three sentences were developed:

Sentence 1: "I retrieve all of my energy bound up in X and take it back to the right place in myself."

Sentence 2: "I remove all non-me energy related to X from all of my cells, from all of my body, and from my personal space, and I send it back to where it truly belongs."

Sentence 3: "I retrieve all of my energy bound up in all of my reactions to X and take it back to the right place in myself."

Willem formed a close working alliance with a small group of psychotherapists, social workers, and coaches, mainly in Switzerland, Italy, and Canada. Together, they explored and analyzed the application in their practices. Over time they added a fourth sentence to bring closure to the issue being resolved: 'I tune all my systems to this new awareness.' They observed a depth of healing and efficiency of results not seen through other methods. The scope of application broadened from trauma to include work on limiting beliefs and fantasies. As the work evolved, the lines between psychology and spirituality blurred. In 2014, the Logosynthesis International Association (LIA) was formed as an international, nonprofit association to support the continuous development of Logosynthesis and quality management of the model.

Stress from the Perspective of Logosynthesis

If we want to enjoy life more fully and live a life with purpose, it is helpful to recap what is happening. We believe we are doing fine because our beliefs tell us that we are right. We recognize that our stress response is activated when things are not as we believe they should be. However, our beliefs tell us that others must change to make our life more comfortable. We react. This energy is activated in response to events around us. Logosynthesis provides a framework to explain this energetic perspective, as outlined in Table 1, on following page.

We are Essence. We come into this world with our life energy in flow and with a purpose. We are spiritual beings having a physical experience, and in order to make sense of the world, we learn through our experiences. Life happens. An event occurs that creates a thought and an emotion. This combination creates energy, which freezes as an imprint. This imprint is a sensory perception such as an image, smell, sound, taste, or touch sensation. It is stored as an energy structure in our personal space—our body and the energetic field that surrounds us. These energy structures are held as beliefs, fantasies, or memories. The greater the intensity of the event, the more highly charged this energy structure and the more energy that is frozen and no longer available to us. Highly traumatic events can freeze significant amounts of energy in the imprint. When a new event occurs, this energy structure is activated, and we react to the initial event rather than to what is happening in the present. As a result, reactions in the present may appear irrational. To change the behavior for future events, we need to access the imprint and release the frozen, or bound, energy. Logosynthesis provides a tested technique to achieve this using the power of words to shift energy.

Table 1

STRESS

A LOGOSYNTHESIS PERSPECTIVE

1 WE ARE BORN WITH LIFE ENERGY IN FLOW.
We are Essence. We come into this life with our energy in flow and with a purpose.

2 LIFE HAPPENS AND EVENTS OCCUR.
We are physical beings and we learn about the world through our experiences.

3 EVENTS TRIGGER A RESPONSE.
We respond to events by producing a thought and an emotion.

4 OUR ENERGY FREEZES.
The energy in this sensory perception freezes as an energy structure.

5 IT IS STORED IN OUR PERSONAL SPACE.
This energy structure is an imprint that is stored in our personal space.

6 WE FORM MEMORIES AND BELIEFS.
Imprints help us make sense of the world by forming our memories and beliefs.

7 A NEW EVENT OCCURS.
Throughout life, we encounter new events and experiences.

8 WE REACT TO THE IMPRINT.
For speed of reaction, we respond not to the new event, but to the initial imprint.

9 WORDS HAVE POWER BEYOND MEANING.
Words have power, beyond their meaning, to shift energy.

10 WE CAN RECONNECT WITH OUR PURPOSE.
The Logosynthesis method releases bound energy. It is now available for our life purpose.

Logosynthesis Offers a Unique Approach

From my experience with Logosynthesis, I know the technique is beautiful and simple, the teachings are deep and profound, and the practice offers a unique approach to health and healing. The more I learn, the more intrigued I become. To date, however, most people have had difficulty comprehending my intense interest. As I ponder why this is so, my heart tells me that we often have a hard time mixing spiritual beliefs with scientific principles. I feel that Logosynthesis is very unique in that it was developed with all the rigor of current scientific knowledge and with a very deep appreciation for the importance of spirit.

 The basis of the work is to help us discover what we are here for in this world and what is keeping us from living our purpose. The following section outlines the key principles of Logosynthesis as it relates to connecting with our life purpose.

A Focus on Our Essence or Spirit

The foundation of Logosynthesis is restoring our natural flow of life energy, Essence, so that it is available for our creative life purpose. The system is based on the following assumptions:

- Loss of awareness of Essence and our task in this world leads to suffering.
- Our awareness of Essence is reduced by frozen parts: perceptions, fantasies, and reactions.
- Frozen parts are rigid energy structures in space rather than abstract concepts.
- The power of words allows us to dissolve these rigid structures and to free our energy for our life task. (Lammers, 2015)

29

To help picture this, we may think of our energy being in a free flow in an open space. An event happens. The combination of the perception (sight, sound, smell, taste, and touch) and the emotion in the moment freezes an imprint, similar to putting up a barricade in the space. The intensity of the event can influence the size of the barricade. Over time, we experience many events and put up many barricades. The space is the space around us, and we no longer have our energy flowing freely. As new events occur that remind us of the original event, we respond based on the past rather than the present. We develop coping mechanisms, which form our personality, to provide us with a certain level of comfort. We may be afraid to let go of these coping mechanisms, especially if we have carried them for a lifetime or if they mask painful memories or traumatic events. Through Logosynthesis, however, our energy is restored to the right place, and our life energy is in flow; it is once again available for fulfilling our life purpose rather than being caught in habitual reactive patterns or stress responses. In other words, Logosynthesis is able to take down the barricades to allow our energy to flow more freely.

A Focus on Our Reaction, Not Our Story

Logosynthesis requires us to acknowledge our emotional reactions. It does not require an analysis of what is causing these feelings or an explanation of how we are coping with or minimizing these feelings. There is no attribution of blame and no need to rationally explain behavior. Simply, we need only to acknowledge the emotions we are experiencing. Is my heart racing or my jaw clenched? Do I feel pain in a certain part of my body? If the distress happened at an earlier point in my life, I simply allow myself to revisit how I felt in the moment.

Often, our rational mind will try to explain our suffering. We can go to great lengths to explain our pain, attribute blame, highlight our coping techniques, and justify our behaviors. We get stuck in a cycle of thinking and doing. We are convinced we know what has caused our current suffering, but the actual emotional imprints are often held outside of our conscious thought. If we can get in touch with our feelings and the associated sensory perceptions, the release may be very quick. We don't alter the event of the past, but we alter the energy structure that it created.

A Focus on the Power of Words to Shift Our Energy

Logosynthesis taps in to the power of spoken words to restore our flow of energy. It applies words and sentences to sensory perceptions to move energy. The sentences used in Logosynthesis contain a manifesting power beyond their meaning. As described above, Willem recognized that the words are connected to a recalled emotional imprint that is associated with a frozen energy structure. In speaking the sentences, energy starts to shift, immediately and beyond reason. The imprint no longer acts as a trigger. We can let go of our urge to react.

As the use of words is a key principle and unique feature of Logosynthesis, I will take some time to emphasize the power of words. The subsequent section describes the three sentences and how they are applied in practice.

I process a lot of words in the run of a day. I speak. I read. I write. I watch. I listen. I recognize that I need to also feel my words. These words carry a vibration. I know my family, friends, and coworkers sense my frustrations through my tone of voice and choice of words. These words manifest based on my emotions. When I align my words with my energy, I can use words to change my beliefs and reactions.

If we look around, there is ample indication that words influence at a deeper level than what we can currently explain. Throughout history, words have been attributed to great power. In spiritual traditions, our world was created using the power of words. We are called to believe and have faith without physical evidence. We use both solitary and group prayer to connect our souls with our god. Leaders use speeches to actively engage people in a shared vision. Words are used to frame thought and to design and invent. They are recognized as having creative power.

We are all familiar with the connection of words and spirit through prayer. In our fast-paced environment, it can be difficult to slow down long enough to connect through prayer. If we aren't disenchanted with the bureaucracy of religion, we may simply be too busy for the rituals and ceremony. We neglect the connection of our prayers with our spiritual health. We can't physically see the effects, so it is very easy to trade the subtle quiet of spirit for the highly noticeable stimuli from our physical world. In many cases, our meals have shifted from a family gathering over blessed food to a solitary snack in front of the television as we browse through messages on our phone. We may have shifted our end-of-day rituals to a few text messages and a quick flick through the news channels rather than kneeling together in prayer. We have so many exciting opportunities for physical and mental stimulation over the course of our day that it becomes very easy to lose the importance of spiritual attention, through words and prayer, in shaping our environment. We tend to neglect the subtle for the obvious.

Although these principles may be difficult for us to fully grasp, they are explained to provide some context to the technique. It is important to emphasize that in a way similar to going to the doctor for medical advice, we do not need to understand how the procedure works to be effective. The work has been developed by a group of experienced professionals with measurable results. If we can accept the process and create a safe space to explore, the results can be very fast and effective.

Chapter 4:
The Logosynthesis Procedure

Logosynthesis is like playing golf. You practice
the same technique every time.
—Willem Lammers, 2015

Create Space to Start

When I was introduced to Logosynthesis, the work was focused on healing trauma and anxiety. My interest was to apply it to help alleviate the stress in my life. I used the books *Logosynthesis - Healing with Words* (Lammers, 2015) and *Self-Coaching with Logosynthesis: How the Power of Words Can Change Your Life* (Lammers, 2015) to help me learn and apply the procedure. The topic was new, so I tried it out.

The technique is the same, whether used by coaches, counselors, or therapists. The same process is followed whether working on relieving the stress of an exam or dealing with post traumatic stress disorder (PTSD). Practicing Logosynthesis requires following a series of specific steps. By repeatedly applying this process, you will be able to more fully appreciate the eloquence of the work. The key to success with Logosynthesis is to learn the technique and apply it consistently and repeatedly to different situations in life. To help you better understand how you can get started on your own, the following steps outline the procedure. It doesn't have to be applied perfectly. Even if you don't understand how it works or if it feels uncomfortable in the beginning, don't worry and keep practicing. The work is subtle, so the results may not always be highly evident in the beginning, but issues and concerns often fall away. Give yourself time and space to explore and learn. The key is to start.

The Step-by-Step Guide

The outline below provided in Table 2 is an overview of the Logosynthesis process. To better illustrate the flow, I will describe each step in detail and according to my experience. As you become familiar with the process, this summary can guide you through the steps.

Table 2

APPLYING THE LOGOSYNTHESIS PROCEDURE

Energy is in flow or it is frozen.
Energy is in the right or wrong space.
Words can move energy.
by Dr. Willem Lammers, 2015

1 BREATHE DEEPLY AND RELAX.
Trust the process.

2 HOW DO YOU REACT OR SUFFER?
What emotions do you feel?
What are the sensations you experience?

3 RATE YOUR LEVEL OF STRESS.
Use a measure for Subjective Units of Distress.

4 NOTICE YOUR SENSORY PERCEPTIONS.
What is happening in the space around you?
Do you notice images, sounds or smells?

5 NAME THE TRIGGER.
Identify the perception using your own words.
Label it 'X'.

6 APPLY THE THREE SENTENCES.
Sentence 1: 'I retrieve all of my energy bound up in 'X'
and take it back to the right place within my Self.'
(Pause)
Sentence 2: 'I remove all non-me energy related to 'X'
from all of my cells, from all of my body and from my
personal space and I send it back to where it truly belongs.'
(Pause)
Sentence 3: 'I retrieve all of my energy bound up in all of
my reactions to 'X' and take it back to the right place in
my Self.'
(Pause)

7 REASSESS YOUR LEVEL OF STRESS.
What is the Subjective Unit of Distress now?
What do you notice about 'X'?

8 CONTINUE OR BRING CLOSURE.
When ready, apply Sentence 4:
'I tune all my systems to this new awareness.'

9 INTEGRATE THE CHANGES IN YOUR LIFE.

Adapted from 'Self-Coaching with Logosynthesis: How the Power of Words
Can Change Your Life' (Dr. Willem Lammers, 2015)

Step 1: Breathe Deeply and Relax

Logosynthesis doesn't require any special tools or high-tech equipment. What it does require may be a little more difficult for most of us to achieve. It requires our attention to quiet our mind and relax. It requires our body and mind to be in a quiet state, allowing us to access our more elusive spirit.

A deep breath can help to settle our "monkey mind"—that busy mind that doesn't stop thinking about all the things on our to-do lists. Creating quiet moments in our favorite spots helps us to sit still. I enjoy waking up an hour earlier than everyone else and going for walks on my own. These moments allow us to get in touch with how we are feeling and to notice what we perceive as we experience these feelings. For many of us, this will be the biggest challenge of the entire process. Our society has trained us to constantly be on the go. The minute we sit still, our minds think of all the things we should be or could be doing. Our bodies respond by taking action, whether it is to put on our running shoes or pick up the remote.

Take note that it may be uncomfortable to acknowledge how we are feeling. As a society, we keep very busy in an effort to suppress our feelings. "Get over it." "Move on." We are conditioned to avoid dealing with feelings. When we slow down to ask how we are doing, uncomfortable feelings arise. Our reaction is to abort the mission and move on to the next thing on our to-do list.

Whether we acknowledge it or not, these feelings produce stress responses. Stress hormones are running rampant through our body as we react to all life's events that come our way. We may even find ourselves thriving on the adrenalin rushes, but don't be fooled. The body's response to chronic stress is well-documented, and it is not healthy. Without a tool to help work through the stresses of life, we are reluctant to allow ourselves to get in touch with the feelings or the events that created them. Over time, it becomes even more difficult to access feelings and sensory perceptions.

There are many ways to get in a zone to relax, but creating a time and place within the daily routine supports this exploration. Breathing deeply and relaxing your body is the critical first step in the Logosynthesis process.

Step 2: How Do You React or Suffer?

Logosynthesis aims to resolve sensory perceptions that create distress and suffering. The second step in the process requires that we acknowledge how we are experiencing stress. We need to admit that we are suffering and recognize how we are suffering. Each of us has our own life story that has created who we are and how we feel.

Getting in touch with how you are experiencing stress is a crucial step. We can suffer physically through pain, pressure, or tension. We can suffer emotionally through fear, grief, shame, or anger. We can kick into a primal fight-or-flight response. We must acknowledge that the acute stress response is a survival mechanism and that chronic stress takes a toll on our health.

As I have become more aware of my stress and the stress of those around me, I have noticed that we can rationalize our stress as a natural part of who we are. While we might know that we are stressed, we may not be willing to recognize how we are experiencing our stress because we know it will take us to a place of discomfort. We need to overcome this hurdle to move forward with Logosynthesis.

As you sit quietly and bring to mind the stressful event, take notice of how your body feels. Are your shoulders tense? Is your mouth dry? Are there any aches or sharp pains you feel? Take note of how your body and your emotions are responding to the stressful event. If you are experiencing discomfort, simply acknowledge what this discomfort feels like. As you tune your attention to your suffering, you may notice an increase in the intensity of the stress. If you feel that you have tapped into the stress, you can move to the next step.

Step 3: Rate Your Level of Stress

After identifying how you feel about the stress, it is important to measure the level of distress.

For many physical interventions, we have precise instruments to measure their impact. At this time, objective measures for Logosynthesis interventions are not readily available. The process therefore uses SUDS, or Subjective Units of Distress Scale, to rate the level of distress on a scale of 0–10. SUDS is a method developed by Joseph Wolpe in 1969 and is used as a tool to measure distress in anxiety disorders and in cognitive behavioral therapy.

Stress is measured in the moment. It is based on your experience. There is no right or wrong answer. The tool is used to provide a benchmark prior to the application of the sentences and will be used after the application of the sentences to assess your new state. This measurement can be done on your own. However, for more complex and intense situations that bring about intense stress responses, it is beneficial to work with a trained practitioner to guide the process.

Step 4: Notice Your Sensory Perceptions

How do we know what is causing our stress? We can't see, hear, or feel events that trigger a stressful reaction. Or can we?

If we allow ourselves to be aware of what we are experiencing in a stressful situation and to notice what we are experiencing in the space around us, we will notice the sensory perceptions, or triggers, that are causing the stressful response. If we tune in to perceptions in our personal space, we will start to notice the distance, direction, and intensity of the trigger. We will start to perceive a visual image or an image through one of our other senses—a smell, a taste, a sound, or a feeling of pressure (touch). The trigger may be also be perceived as a memory, fantasy, symbol, or another form. We will start to sense things in our personal space.

Step 5: Name the Trigger

You may not cognitively understand or be able to provide a rational explanation for the sensations you are experiencing, but this is the realm of feeling and sensation, so it is important to allow the sensations to flow. Don't analyze or explain. Do not rush this process. You may not be able to access the triggers right away. Triggers can be complex, and it may not be possible to get to a root event in one Logosynthesis session. Simply pick something that resonates with you. Be sure to pay attention to the sensory perceptions rather than your feelings tied to the perceptions. Frame the trigger in words that can be inserted into the Logosynthesis sentences.

Step 6: Apply the Three Sentences

As our brains are trained to fix things, it is tempting to jump to this step right away. We may be in a rush to apply the sentences to what we think is causing our stress. It is very easy to use our rational brain to sort through events in our past that must have resulted in emotional imprints and now affect our behavior and levels of stress.

But Logosynthesis is based in energy work rather than rational thought process. Our conscious thought does not access our subconscious levels (as shown in studies of people who claim they are not racist yet behave in racist ways). It is important to spend time in the earlier steps of Logosynthesis to access the feelings that drive our behavior. If we approach the sentences with our cognitive brain, we will not achieve the desired results.

As discussed above, it is imperative to be open to the power of words in allowing the release of energy bound in our personal space. The same three sentences are used each time and will become familiar with practice.

1. I retrieve all of my energy bound up in X (person, object, event, place, or aspects thereof) and take it back to the right place in my Self.
   – Processing pause (pause … let go … let it work …)

2. I remove all non-me energy related to X (frozen form of person, object, event, place, or any aspect of these) from all of my cells, from all of my body, and from my personal space and send it back to where it truly belongs.
   – Processing pause (pause … let go … let it work …)

3. I retrieve all of my energy bound up in all of my reactions to X (frozen form of person, object, event, place, or any aspect thereof) and take it back to the right place in my Self.
   – Processing pause (pause … let go … let it work …)

During the application of the sentences, you may notice sensations as the energy releases. Flickering eyelashes, an opening of the chest, or yawning are common. Allow your body to respond and the energy to flow.

Step 7: Reassess Your Level of Stress

Taking time to recognize changes is an important step in the process. After applying the sentences, allow sufficient time for the processing to work, and once again subjectively assess your level of stress on the same scale of 0–10.

In most cases, the level of distress will diminish, and you can expect to feel calmer. The measure may not start at ten and may not drop to zero. The second assessment allows you to determine if further work to reduce the stress is warranted. At this point, notice again the space around you for sensory perceptions and acknowledge any sensations that you may have noticed in the pauses between the Logosynthesis sentences. In many cases, the sentences and subsequent processing will identify a deeper level to which another set of sentences can be applied. The work may also uncover new sensations from past experiences.

Allowing the sensations to come to the forefront may be easier with the assistance of a Logosynthesis guide, but it is important to acknowledge the feelings that arise as opposed to thinking about and rationally explaining why a particular feeling or thought appeared.

Step 8: Continue or Bring Closure

At this point in the process, you can determine if you are satisfied with how you are feeling. If there is a sense that the issue has been resolved and you want to bring closure to the topic, a fourth sentence can be applied:

I tune all of my systems to this new awareness.

If you feel further work would be beneficial, you can repeat the process or wait for a later time.

Due to the complexity of the emotional imprints related to past events, it may be difficult to assess if issues are fully resolved. The key to Logosynthesis is not in analyzing the stress, but in identifying and releasing the triggers that cause you to feel stress. As the emotional imprint or trigger is released, you can bring closure to the event and its stress response.

Step 9: Integrate the Changes in Your Life

Anytime we let go of old patterns of behavior and make changes in our lives, we need to assess how we incorporate new behaviors. For example, if we let go of the stress of persistently needing to be busy and no longer feel the urge to be working constantly, how do we fill our time, achieve our goals, and interact with those around us?

As explained earlier, Logosynthesis is founded on gaining alignment with our Essence or life force. It is imperative to tune in to Essence and your true Self to guide your life journey.

The goal of Logosynthesis is to let go of trauma and stress that is no longer serving you and to allow yourself to be open to finding true meaning and purpose in your life. Applying the process not only to painful, traumatic memories, but also to limiting beliefs and future fears, can help guide your development. The method can provide therapeutic benefits and a spiritual perspective to help you to realize your full potential.

These are changes that happen from within you. Others will not be able to physically see the changes that you are making. Do not expect others to readily recognize your efforts or results. I have learned to not require their recognition or acceptance, whereas in the past, I required the approval and appreciation of others to fuel my motivation. I am now content to continue on my path in my own way. That's okay. I'm okay.

The Empty Chair Exercise

It is difficult to appreciate this material through reading alone. At this point, it may be beneficial to actually try the method. The empty chair exercise is a technique used in the Logosynthesis basic training that allows you to start experiencing how a shift in energy might feel.

In training, Dr. Lammers uses the empty chair exercise. We are guided to think of someone who has mildly annoyed or irritated us and place the person in an imaginary chair. This is not an exercise in thinking of a highly emotional relationship. It is meant to allow you to notice your subtle energy, often felt through the core of your body. For most of us, this takes some guidance because we have been conditioned to avoid these feelings. However, this is a necessary first step in the process. Our tendency may be to go directly to the issue, deal with it, and move on, but often, we may not be ready to deal with it at this point. Energy shifts may be quite dramatic, and it is advised that we become familiar with the technique and seek the guidance of a practitioner to work through more intense feelings.

We can experiment with the steps as follows:

Relax and focus on your breathing.

Imagine an empty chair.

Imagine a person in this chair who annoys or irritates you, for whatever reason.

Measure the level of distress on a scale of 0–10. This will be your SUDS rating.

Assess any sensory perceptions around you in the form of a visual image, sound, taste, or smell.

Apply the sentences to the sensory perception:

I retrieve all my energy bound in the representation of the person sitting in the chair and take it back to the right place within my Self.

Processing pause.

I remove all non-me energy related to the representation of the person sitting in the chair from all of my cells, from all of my body and from my personal space and send it back to where it truly belongs.

Processing pause.

I retrieve all of my energy bound up in all of my reactions to the representation of the person sitting in the chair and take it back to the right place within my Self.

Processing pause.

Now assess your emotions, body sensations, or thoughts toward this person on a distress scale of 0–10.

What has shifted or changed?

Through this process, you will notice how you feel emotions. You will also notice the sensory perceptions imprinted from the individual as you apply the sentences to the imprint. This is all in the realm of energy. As you start to notice this energy, it becomes easier to access other emotional imprints that may be causing you to react.

Chapter 5: Applying Logosynthesis

Recognizing how I feel my stress and identifying the sensory perceptions that I experience during stressful episodes allows me to release triggers.

Sharing Stories for Learning

We learn through stories of how individuals apply the technique so that we can understand how it can benefit us in our personal lives. To date, most of the work has been developed in the area of counselor-client or therapist-patient relationship around trauma and anxiety. *Letting It Go. Relieve Anxiety and Toxic Stress in Just a Few Minutes Using Only Words* (Weiss, 2016) provides a great instructional approach to applying the technique. As we continue to strive to better cope with our challenges and to maximize our opportunities, we can discover further application to help live our lives more fully. I have applied Logosynthesis in numerous everyday situations, both for myself and with friends. I believe it is helpful to illustrate the principles of Logosynthesis in the context of these stories.

Over the past few years, I have embraced Logosynthesis as a personal development tool. To start, I read any material I could find (which was very limited). I pondered the topic, but I didn't know anyone who could answer my questions. I can't say my attempts in Logosynthesis were transformational. I periodically picked up the book and applied the sentences to what I felt were my triggers to my reactive behavior. I could tell there was something to the method, but I wanted more information.

On a whim, in April 2015, I signed up for the Logosynthesis Basics course. I had to set aside some important commitments that weekend, and I was definitely pushing outside my comfort zone, but I went anyway. I set aside three days with a small group to learn about the theory and apply the method.

I was blown away.

Everyone noticed results, often much more profound than they could have anticipated. The weekend learning renewed my energy and my interest in figuring out Logosynthesis. It also helped me recognize the important role of trained practitioners in guiding the process. From that course forward, I have integrated this method into my life, whether enjoying a peaceful paddle on the lake, a relaxing walk in nature, or a quiet moment with an early-morning cup of coffee. I will share a few examples of my early discoveries so that you can gain a better understanding of Logosynthesis and how you can easily start now to apply it in your life. As you expand your learning, I am convinced you will continue to be intrigued!

Losing My Cool as a Parent

I was thirty-five when my first daughter was born. I was excited about becoming a mother. I was busy with work and house renovations, but I was now ready to parent. I felt I had things under control. While friends were experiencing sleepless nights and overwhelming stress around being new mothers, I felt relaxed and calm. We continued to do almost everything we had done before. Even after my second daughter was born sixteen months later, I felt I had things under control. Aside from routine naps, we just incorporated the girls into our schedules. We hosted dinner parties while they slept. We timed our road trips around their nap times. I put them in a double stroller if I wanted to go for a run. I had parenting under control, and I made it look pretty easy.

But then, around the age of three, my daughters started to flex their independence. They decided they didn't like the vegetables that I prepared for their supper. They didn't want to wear the pretty dresses I had set out for them, changing at the last minute before we headed out the door. They didn't play together with their dolls as nicely as I wanted. Because I was the mother, I knew it was my responsibility to teach them, but the more I flexed my control, the more they pushed back. I no longer had the patience for parenting, and I was blessed to have a few friends at a similar parenting stage to empathize with and to console me. Yet, it did not feel right to me. I wanted to be a calm parent, and, inside, I was not calm.

I will note at this point that I could rationally explain my behavior to myself and to others. I was the parent, and in the moment, I strongly believed that my daughters should have known better. I may have acknowledged to myself that I was overreacting at times, but I figured that if I had already told them to do something several times, I was going to reinforce the message even if I was frustrated. I wanted to be calmer, but I was not willing to be a pushover.

With my initial introduction to Logosynthesis, I sensed that this was the tool to help me end the reactive cycle of losing my cool. I read the material, and despite the focus on dealing with trauma, it resonated. If I could find what was triggering this stress, I might be able to change my behavior. I tried the technique on my own and sensed I was on to something, but I was still losing my cool. I felt I needed some guidance, so I worked up the courage to approach Trish North, a psychotherapist trained in Logosynthesis. Even for me, already very open to personal development, a session with a psychotherapist was not a quick decision. However, my curiosity got the better of me. My goal was that in a one-hour session, I would be able to pinpoint the emotional imprint that caused me to get frustrated with my children. Life would be good.

As I sat in her office, I explained why I was there and that I wanted to learn the technique. Trish very calmly listened, trying to get to know me and understand my motivation for learning Logosynthesis. I just needed her to tell me what I had to do. I would do it and be on my way.

I told her that I consistently got frustrated, and despite knowing it wasn't the right thing to do, I continued to repeat the same behavior. In my attempt to explain this to her, I started to ramble off a list of examples. She encouraged me to think of a specific incident when I had lost my patience. I paused.

I picked a time when I confronted the girls about arguing with each other. They had been upstairs, and I could hear them arguing, so I marched upstairs to find one shutting the door of her room in front of the other. Well, that wasn't appropriate. I was angry. Trish asked me to describe the sensation of getting angry.

I had been caught up in explaining my story. Now, I had to pause and describe how I knew I was angry in that moment when I approached this specific situation with my daughters. How did I feel? I had to take note. I could bring myself to feel a tension in my chest and throat area that I had felt at the time of the argument.

Trish asked me to spend a moment in that situation, noticing what was happening. She then asked me to rate, on a scale of 0–10, the level of this distress. I believe I rated it an eight.

Next, she asked me to notice any images or sounds. I am not a visual person and I understand that, during Logosynthesis, most people will see images of people or events. I was struggling to describe what I noticed. Trish sat quietly, asked what came to mind, and probed whether I was able to describe what I was sensing. It was the face of my daughter as she closed the door to shut out her sister. This was an imprint. Because I didn't see the visual image, I was having some difficulty sensing where this imprint was located in my personal space. Trish guided me to stay focused on locating it. I sensed it was right in front of me. Trish quietly told me she had a sentence for me, which I was to repeat after her.

I retrieve all of my energy ... bound in the representation ... of my daughter closing the door ... and send it back to the right place within myself.

I sat quietly for about two minutes. Nothing really happened other than that I could feel my eyes flickering a bit. I looked at Trish. She gave me the next sentence.

I remove all non-me energy ... bound in the representation of my daughter closing the door ... from my cells, my body and my personal space ... and I send it back to where it truly belongs.

Again I sat quietly for several minutes. Nothing much happened. Again, I was aware of some eye movement and perhaps some yawning. I could feel my chest getting a bit lighter, but it was nothing earth-shattering. I looked at Trish, and she gave me the next sentence.

I retrieve all my energy ... bound in all my reactions ... to the representation of my daughter closing the door ... and I send it back to the right place within myself.

Another pause, much the same as the last two pauses. After several minutes, Trish asked me gently what was happening when I thought of approaching the situation now. I was not as agitated. I subjectively assigned a stress level of four. She asked me what I now noticed. Not much. It did not seem very dramatic, but it felt as though something subtle was happening. I had experienced similar situations with my sisters when we were children, even though we knew it was not appropriate behavior. The distress had shifted from eight to four, and I felt calmer when I reflected on the incident, so we wrapped up the session.

I continued to be aware of my reactions to my daughters when they didn't do things the right way. They were hard workers and eager to please. Yet when the floor wasn't swept the way I had instructed or the dishes weren't done properly, it didn't matter how deeply I breathed. I would inevitably express my displeasure. Two girls would be standing there saying, "I'm sorry." I knew there was something triggering this behavior that I wasn't getting at, and I was determined to find it.

One evening in May 2015, shortly after I had completed the Logosynthesis basic training, I sat on the dock and soaked in the sunset over the lake. I allowed myself to explore my reactions when the girls didn't do what they were told. I allowed myself to feel what was happening in these situations. Why do I have to tell them things over and over again? I shouldn't have to tell them every time. I could feel a tension in my chest. As I brought to mind various situations, the tension in my chest increased. I rated the level of distress around an eight. Why couldn't they sweep the floor the way they were told? A childhood storybook titled *Little Mommy* popped into my mind. These words repeated in my head, "This is my house and I am the Mommy. My children are Annabelle, Betsy and Bonnie. They are good little children and do just as I say." Was this the imprint? Where was this located in my personal space? I could sense the book, which had the cover torn off from excessive reading, but I didn't have a strong image. I could hear the words, "They are good little children and do just as I say." I struggled a bit to sense exactly where this representation was located. I felt that was located to my right. I decided to apply the sentences.

I retrieve all of my energy ... bound in the words ... "They are good little children and do just as I say" ... and send it back to the right place within myself.

I sat quietly soaking in the fresh, spring air. I didn't notice a lot. I felt a lightening sensation in my chest—a subtle, expansive lifting sensation. It was a beautiful sunset, and I was not in a rush, so I sat quietly a little longer.

I remove all non-me energy ... bound in the words ... "They are good little children and do just as I say" ... from my cells, my body and my personal space ... and I send it back to where it truly belongs.

I noticed a bit of flickering eye movement but really not much. Quiet. There was no need for me to rush.

I retrieve all my energy ... bound in all my reactions to the words ... "They are good little children and do just as I say" ... and I send it back to the right place within myself.

I reflected back on being a young girl with this little book, dreaming of having such pretty dolls in pretty dresses and picturing what life should be like for a little mommy. I sensed that my energy was bound in this imprint, a fantasy of what my life should be like based on a 1960s stereotype that bore no resemblance to my routines. I knew that only time could tell if this processing would have an effect, so one month later, after cleaning the house, I made note there was no yelling and no frustration, even when I noticed a dusty spot that should have been swept. Calm. Peaceful.

My rational mind tells me it is stupid to think that a sentence from a book that I had as a child could cause me to lose my temper as a parent forty-five years later. But if I sense the meaning behind this little story, it depicted a lifestyle that was pretty, calm, and predictable. The representation of that cute little girl surrounded with her pretty dolls "doing just as I say" told me this is how my life should be. Regardless of the explanation, after ten years of trying to break the habit of losing my temper with my daughters, I finally feel that a significant trigger to my reactions is gone. This highlights that although we all may react to our children's behavior, we all have our own frozen energy structures that are triggering our reaction, and we all have to use our own words to neutralize our reactions. I was not aware of my trigger until I created the space to apply this process. This is consistent with what I have seen with others who have applied the technique, and I suspect you will be surprised with what comes to your awareness when you follow the outlined procedure.

I have come to realize there is not one trigger for all my reactions. My unique life experiences and my cultural beliefs are a source of many triggers. I now take note of behaviors and reactions that are not appropriate as they occur. At the end of the day or when an opportunity arises, I apply the technique. I notice that, in some cases, my reactions may not disappear completely, but the intensity or frequency may be less. In other cases, I no longer feel an urge to react when something happens. Over time, I have noticed that my energy has shifted so that I am less reactive. Yes, I have work to do, but I feel like I am making significant progress.

Managing Stress at Work

Most of us find that our workplaces can be sources of stress. Demands are high, and the environment may not be comfortable to us. Logosynthesis can be a useful technique to help us recognize our reactions and identify our triggers so that we can shift our energy and create a more productive work environment. Rather than constantly reacting to the urgent tasks that fill our day, we can better focus on the jobs that are important for overall success.

My family jokes that the need to voice our opinion is a Lammers trait passed down from my mother's large family. At home and at work, I have an opinion on just about everything. Because I work for a large organization, it can be challenging to determine when it is important to support corporate initiatives and when to voice concerns about their impact at my level. I have always had a strong belief that it is imperative to voice my opinions and highlight any concerns so that pragmatic decisions can be made.

Several years ago, the company I work for acknowledged that there was a lot of administrative work for people in my role across the organization, and it was well-communicated that management had heard our concerns and was committed to simplification. New roles were created, consultants were hired, and systems were put in place to allow us more time to spend on strategic selling and customer focus. Without fail, however, the well-intentioned initiatives created more work or slowed us down. I was diligent in objectively explaining to management what was happening and how we were becoming overwhelmed with simplification and that we were collectively done with simplification.

Much to my surprise, the terminology then changed to *decomplexity*. As my children quickly pointed out, this is just a more complicated way of saying simplification. I felt the need to highlight this point to the project lead, and at the same time, I was being asked to comment on what the leadership team had outlined under the strategic pillar of simplification. A new aspect to the issue was added as the company was purchased and new leadership was announced.

As I sat at home early one morning thinking about how to craft my input into the simplification discussion, I noticed I was getting increasingly distraught about the entire stream of events. As I started to type, I could feel my frustration level rise, with my teeth clenching. I thought I would head out to the hot tub to apply Logosynthesis and try to pinpoint my distress. As I allowed myself to feel the stress and recognize my sensory perceptions around the stress, what came to mind was quite interesting. I perceived being a kid in a hayfield, and everyone around me was busy. I was trying to keep up with the pace, but I was having difficulty. Next, I spent a few moments trying to locate this representation in my personal space. The hay wagon, filled with people, was in front of me. I think that for most people, this sort of sensation would appear in the form of images. For me, it appeared more of as an intuitive perception or a representation. I applied the sentences using the word *representation* rather than *image*, but I think both would have had the effect.

I retrieve all of my energy … bound in the representation of the hay wagon with everyone on board … and send it back to the right place within myself.

I paused and closed my eyes. The June morning was quiet and calm, so I took my time to let the energy shift.

I remove all non-me energy ... bound in the representation of the hay wagon with everyone on board ... from my cells, my body and my personal space ... and I send it back to where it truly belongs.

Another pause. I did not force any thoughts or analyze the situation.

I retrieve all my energy ... bound in all my reactions to the representation of the hay wagon with everyone on board ... and I send it back to the right place within myself.

Hmmm ... Next, I perceived running after the hay wagon, trying to get on and join the rest of the gang. I realized that I couldn't keep up. I applied the sentences to this perception.

I retrieve all of my energy ... bound in the representation of running after the hay wagon ... and send it back to the right place within myself.

Pause. Breathe.

I remove all non-me energy ... bound in the representation of running after the hay wagon ... from my cells, my body, and my personal space ... and I send it back to where it truly belongs.

Quiet.

I retrieve all my energy ... bound in all my reactions to the representation of running after the hay wagon ... and I send it back to the right place within myself.

I let the wagon go on with everyone on board, and I just sat there. I realized that it was okay. I sensed that I didn't have to get on the wagon, and I would be just fine. Hmm ... I'm not sure exactly what it meant, but for me, it seemed to release the need to keep up with everything and have input into everything. I can still work hard and be committed to my role, but the wagon will go on regardless and that's okay.

At work, I noticed that I still offered input, but my energy had shifted so that I didn't have the same compelling need to have my say. And when I did voice my opinion, I sensed the energy around it was somewhat different. However, I continued to react to situations, and

I continued to assess what I was reacting to on a regular basis. From there, I would identify the imprint, apply the sentences, and allow time for the energy to shift.

There was a lot happening in our office. A customer went out of business, meaning that two junior employees (with young families) were without a client. Some of the work transferred to my desk, adding to an already heavy workload. My idea was to call our director of HR to request that my desk be split into two and that they keep the two employees and let me go.

In August, the new management announced a major restructure. With no explanation, fifteen-minute meetings were scheduled for the following day to inform a large number of colleagues that their employment was being terminated. I received a meeting notice for nine. I had been giving thought to what my life would be like if my employment were to be terminated. I faced the meeting with excitement rather than fear. I felt that the work pertaining to the hay wagon going on without me had really helped to dissolve any stress associated with the upcoming event. I felt ready for the meeting.

Oddly, due to a last-minute change, I still had my job. I was not sure how I felt. A few days later, I decided to apply Logosynthesis again. I went back to my perception of the hayfield. I thought the wagon had come around the field, and I had to get back on—but this time, there were a lot fewer people on the wagon. I felt I should drive the tractor rather than get on the wagon, but that was not an option. I could get on and decide whether I sat quietly on my bale of hay or whether I engaged with the group and made the most of it. I know my personality leans toward the latter, but I felt disengaged at that point and just wanted to sit alone and be quiet. I would do what I was asked and move a bale when necessary, but I was not interested in building the load or interfering with their plans because that was not what they wanted.

I was getting back on a very different wagon. The wagon took a very big jolt, and a lot of people fell off; the ones who remained were visibly shaken. The chatter and camaraderie had stopped. Everyone was sullen.

I assessed my stress and noticed the sensory perception of this new representation of the hay wagon. I said each of the sentences using this new representation.

I retrieve all of my energy ... bound in the representation of the hay wagon ... and send it back to the right place within myself.

Pause.

I remove all non-me energy ... bound in representation of the hay wagon ... from my cells, my body and my personal space ... and I send it back to where it truly belongs.

Another pause. I did not force any thoughts or analyze the situation.

I retrieve all my energy ... bound in all my reactions to the representation of the hay wagon ... and I send it back to the right place within myself.

I sat quietly, but I could feel my energy shifting through the core of my body. It didn't take long for things to settle a bit. I was now ready to get back to work.

Frustration in a Relationship

Relationships can bring us joy, but they can also be stressors because of our beliefs about those relationships. Also, each of us in the relationship brings our history with our individual past experiences and our culture, which have created our beliefs. When we first meet, we get to know each other by discussing common interests and sharing new experiences. We look for areas of shared values for a foundation and discuss shared visions for a framework. However, as our relationships progress, we start to experience some discomfort when things don't get done quite the way we expected or at a pace that suits our liking. We may not want to make a big deal about it, but almost automatically, we throw a look or think a thought that gets noticed. When the behavior repeats, our reactions repeat, and we begin a cycle of acting and reacting.

While I was working on maintaining my cool as a parent and keeping my stress in check at work, I also realized I could use some focus on my relationship with my husband. I am blessed with a very supportive partner. We share a lot of important values around family, work, and lifestyle. I don't question his decisions in the areas of money and finance and I don't think he spends much energy questioning mine. We want for nothing, so nothing should bother me, right? Life should be wonderful.

Yet, I was finding myself frustrated with some of the little things. I knew there was no reason to be stressed out, so I felt guilty at being petty. I didn't really say a lot; I just stomped around in a bad mood when things weren't done my way. It became a habitual pattern that I was having difficulty breaking. I didn't like feeling this way, and I didn't want to make a big deal about it, so I decided to explore these reactions using Logosynthesis.

Where should I start? The technique begins with the question, "How do you suffer or stress?" or as I reference, "What bothers me?" I knew I became stressed when I took everything on and tried to do it all—work all day, come home to cook supper and take the girls to their sporting activities, pick up some groceries while out, and when finally home again, clean the kitchen and throw in a load of laundry. I knew what had to be done, and I did it. Did I need help? Sure, but I was not going to nag or even ask for help. I could do it all.

What was I feeling? Frustration. How did that feel? I could bring myself to feel the sensation of pressure rising in my head, with my jaws clenching and my face tightening. I could work up my frustration level quite easily. Next, I rated the level of stress on a scale of 0–10. I recognized that it wasn't severe or debilitating, but definitely strong. I rated it at a six.

What did I notice when I experienced this feeling? I struggled a little to locate the sensory perception or emotional imprint. I took my time to notice what appeared for me. I heard the words, "I shouldn't have to tell you what to do," "You should be able to see what needs to be done and do it," and "It's not my job to tell you what needs to be done." I followed the Logosynthesis steps, and rather than analyze why I was hearing these words, I accepted the words as the imprint and applied the sentences.

I retrieve all of my energy ... bound in the words "I shouldn't have to tell you what to do" ... and send it back to the right place within myself.

I allowed time to process this. I found myself repeating this sentence before progressing to the next.

I remove all non-me energy ... bound in the words "I shouldn't have to tell you what to do" ... from my cells, my body and my personal space ... and I send it back to where it truly belongs.

I could feel some relief in my head.

I retrieve all my energy ... bound in all my reactions to the words "I shouldn't have to tell you what to do" ... and I send it back to the right place within myself.

As the third sentence processed, I noticed that the intensity with which I said this sentence subsided. I rated my stress level more as a three or four.

I had been taking on the workload without asking for help. My reactions to the imprint were not at all helpful because the stomping around did not encourage support, but rather avoidance. Actually, if I was struggling through something and someone asked if I wanted any help, my reaction was definitely not a, "Yes, please," but rather a curt

"I've got it." You can probably understand that my family responded by doing something else rather than pitching in and risking another similar remark.

These days, I still tend to take on too much, but I don't feel that same level of frustration, and I am less likely to snap back when help is offered. I am better able to ask for help. I still have some work to do, but I feel much better equipped to manage the chatter of the inner voice that triggers many of my reactions.

Physical Reactions to Hidden Memories

As I explore Logosynthesis to help me manage stress and reduce my reactions, I appreciate the ease of application and the shift in my energy. I feel better. I am quite convinced that my friends would benefit from this work as well, but I know that, first, they have to be open to the idea. Second, I have to be in the right space to offer it. I am not a qualified therapist, but I do have a lot of conversations with friends. I would like to incorporate this technique into our conversations so that rather than commiserate about things that stress us out, we could start to identify the imprints and apply the sentences to reduce our stress.

One beautiful June evening, I dropped the girls off for basketball practice and headed out to run a few errands. A friend, Alison, happened to be out for a walk while her daughter was at a nearby soccer practice, so she joined me for the drive. I inquired about her day, and she explained that she had had a presentation that didn't go as planned. As a result, she'd had a pounding headache since midday. We talked about how things transpired. In short, she had been challenged in front of a group of clients to defend the numbers in her presentation. She knew she was right, and on the outside, she held her composure. Inside, she was far from calm. Her client indicated that she was going to double-check her numbers while my friend continued her presentation. The client returned forty-five minutes later, apologizing for the confusion. Alison's presentation wrapped up just fine, but her pounding headache persisted as the day wore on.

Alison and I had discussed Logosynthesis previously, but she said she hadn't been able to get the hang of it. Since we were waiting for the girls and had some time, and since I had recently completed the basic workshop, I offered to guide her through the process. She agreed. We started with what she was feeling—her pounding head. On a level of distress, she rated it an eight. I asked her if she noticed any images. She took her time to assess. There was an image of a black hole in front of her, she said. We decided to start with that, and I paid special attention to use her specific words. It had to be her imprint, not my version of her imprint.

I retrieve all of my energy ... bound in the image of the black hole in front of me ... and send it back to the right place within myself.

I drove. She was quiet for a few minutes.

I remove all non-me energy ... bound in the image of the black hole in front of me ... from my cells, my body and my personal space ... and I send it back to where it truly belongs.

I noticed her facial expression shift.

I retrieve all my energy ... bound in all my reactions to image of the black hole in front of me ... and I send it back to the right place within myself.

Alison said she felt an easing as the sentences processed. I asked her how she was doing and whether she had noticed a shift. She said she now felt the level of stress was more like a five.

We thought we were doing pretty well. We had assessed how she felt, identified an imprint, and applied the sentences. The post assessment indicated some reduction in the level of stress. We were actually quite proud of ourselves. We arrived back at the school and still had some extra time before the practices were over, so we chatted a bit. It seemed as though there was more to the pounding head, so I asked if she wanted to explore it a bit more. She was interested and we revisited the pounding head, now at a level of five. She said she noticed an image of something totally unrelated—the image of the brick wall of her elementary school. Well, according to the protocol, we were not to analyze this imprint but rather apply the sentences. So I had her repeat after me.

I retrieve all of my energy ... bound in the image of the brick wall of my elementary school ... and send it back to the right place within myself.

Pause.

I remove all non-me energy ... bound in the image of the brick wall of my elementary school ... from my cells, my body and my personal space ... and I send it back to where it truly belongs.

Pause.

I retrieve all my energy ... bound in all my reactions to the image of the brick wall of my elementary school ... and I send it back to the right place within myself.

Pause.

I could tell by Alison's facial expressions that there had been an energy shift. After several minutes, she explained that she had a memory from when she was five or six years old and had been playing with a group of boys. One was swinging her around and just happened to let her go. She went flying into the brick wall and was knocked out. As she regained consciousness, she was unable to remember anything. The next image to work with through the sentences was "the brick wall right in front of me." Together, we went through the Logosynthesis steps again. As the sentences processed during the pauses, the image of the wall moved back, and the pounding in her head eased. After she had finished the third sentence, she explained her memory that the principal had come out, held her, and demanded she identify who had been swinging her. She had no recollection at the time, but was eventually forced to pick someone out of the crowd. She just wanted the pain to stop and wanted everyone to stop looking at her as they waited for the answer. As she spoke, she realized that this was very similar to what she experienced earlier in the day. She wanted everyone to stop looking at her as they waited for the answer. Her headache was now gone.

Alison acknowledged that she had always felt some guilt that she had probably picked the wrong boy that day. There may have been more that we could have worked on, but that seemed like quite enough for a Friday evening. We let it go at that point. We were a little stunned at how it all unfolded. In the length of time we would normally carry on a conversation, she was able to resolve a pounding head. We were both amazed at how quickly the process worked. Without trying to recall a series of past events that may or may not have caused her reaction, she simply acknowledged her feelings and noticed any sensory perceptions. As soon as the imprint was identified, the sentences could be applied. The entire process was probably in the range of thirty minutes, and at the end, she felt fine, reportedly followed by a very good sleep that night. I am not a trained practitioner, but I simply created a safe, comfortable space and helped Alison follow the steps.

Chapter 6: Overcoming Barriers to Logosynthesis

The technique is simple, but the work is powerful. I have learned to take it easy and appreciate the journey.

Identifying Barriers to the Technique

Logosynthesis is a beautifully simple practice that I believe can transform the way you react to life. As with any new process, however, it is important to be aware of potential barriers and to identify helpful tips to guide you as you learn the technique. This section will describe some stumbling blocks that I have encountered so that you can recognize them as they occur and work through the inevitable challenges of implementing techniques to change your habits, reactions, and behaviors.

I Can't Get in the Zone

For many of us, every hour of every day is planned and accounted for. We rush from one activity or commitment to the next. We get agitated when people tell us to slow down or take a break. Our rational thinking confirms that we are busy because everything is important and urgent. When we finally slow down, we become uncomfortable and quickly find something to occupy our time. This is a good place to start with Logosynthesis.

Notice what you are feeling when you sit quietly. Become aware of your inner chatter. Notice the words and phrases that come to mind. Identify your sensory perceptions, and start to apply the sentences. Maybe there is a reason you can't relax. Perhaps you can start to let go of your need to always keep busy and active. Don't force things. Just be aware and willing to try something a little different.

It Doesn't Make Sense

I have had a lot of conversations about Logosynthesis, I have shared the self-coaching book, and I have discussed the topic through a blog. I commonly hear that people are open to the idea, but they don't understand the process or can't grasp how saying a few sentences could change behavior. Logosynthesis is a very simple approach, but we can't understand it solely through reading or hearing about it. As with any technique, we gain understanding through practice and experience. We learn through doing.

Interestingly, we don't have to understand all the details for the process to work. We just need to trust that the process works. We trust that surgeons and dentists have been trained with skills to help us. We have to place similar trust in Logosynthesis practitioners and in the process. Although this work requires a shift in our thinking, it is based on age-old spiritual wisdom that encourages us to believe without having seen.

I Believe My Stress Is Under Control

With any form of change, the initial step is to realize the need for change. We have been trained to suppress any stress and anxiety, usually through adopting coping strategies and avoiding acknowledgement of our feelings. From a very early age, we are coached to not be a crybaby, to play tough, and not to let our opponents see any weakness. We feel that if we ignore the thoughts or push away the memories, we can avoid the pain or the stress. When stress and anxiety surface through negative feelings (shame, anger, fear, or guilt), unexplained behaviors (fight or flight) or hurtful thoughts, we engage in activities that reduce the discomfort. We then feel that we have our stress under control.

I would pose that this only suppresses our stress. The danger is that we can never be sure when it will emerge in a manner that causes damage to our relationships or ourselves. Think of the difference between these two sentences: "I have my stress under control," and "I do not feel stressed." We need to approach Logosynthesis with the intent of dissolving our stress rather than simply controlling it. To do so, we first have to relax our mind and body and actually feel our stress.

I Can't Access the Imprints

Just as we are trained not to notice our feelings, we may also have difficulty noticing our sensory perceptions and emotional imprints. We have five senses that can provide us with inputs: sight, hearing, taste, smell, and touch. Many people perceive visually. They see images of people, places, and things and can easily locate these in their personal space. The sentences can be applied as the images arise. Others do not see images but find that sounds or smells trigger powerful reactions. Although perhaps a little harder to recognize, people react to touch and feel. I stay focused on what I am noticing and work with the words, sounds, and representations that come to mind. It can be extremely helpful to consult trained professionals in Logosynthesis to guide you through this step of the process.

It's Not Me Who Has to Change

It is common to feel we're not the ones who have to change, but we react to others in ways that are damaging both to us and to them. Releasing the energy bound in our beliefs means the actions of others no longer bother us and that there is not a constant feeling of needing to control our reactions. We no longer need to work as hard to control the actions of others and have our energy available to focus on things that are important to us. In many cases, it allows us to approach our challenges from a better position so that others will be able to better understand us.

It is always me who has to change. The change must come from within, and any negative reactions are merely indicators that there is work to be done to better accept things as they are. Only then can we create space to be present for our purpose.

I Am Scared About What Will Be Uncovered

From a very early age, we are encouraged to be in control. Control your destiny. Control your emotions. However, we are often fooled into thinking we are in control when in reality, emotional triggers affect our behavior in ways that our cognitive minds do not understand. The fear of letting go and uncovering painful memories or embarrassing fantasies is very understandable. Part of my initial interest in Logosynthesis related to the ability to do it on my own and not share any part of myself or explain any of my behaviors to others. I do recognize that many people suffer from significant anxiety from traumatic events in their life. In some cases, Logosynthesis work can be intense and overwhelming. If you have concerns about working through difficult situations, I highly recommend that you get professional support to guide you. There is a list of certified practitioners on the Logosynthesis website (www.logosynthesis.international). We are not meant to face all our difficulties and challenges on our own.

I'm Not Getting the Results I Want

We are trained to measure success based on what we do and what we see. But we will not always notice our energy has shifted, and our response has changed. As I engage in conversations using the Logosynthesis process, I notice that people do let go of what is bothering them. In some cases, they do not even realize what has happened, but in follow-up conversations, it is apparent that what was bothering them no longer is a stressor. The issue appears to just fall away.

I Can't Fit into a Routine

If you are like most people, you have a long to-do list. We are geared to perform in a high-stimulus society. We work harder, run faster, party better, volunteer more hours, sleep less—and the list goes on. When we do slow down for quiet time, there is often an uneasy feeling that causes us to gear up rather than slow down. The fact that you may find Logosynthesis boring or can't fit it into your routine is not a surprise. The good news is that it doesn't have to be boring and can easily fit into your daily routine. Like meditation, Logosynthesis involves accessing our spirit or our energy. Unlike many meditations, Logosynthesis offers a very specific procedure to identify the triggers to our stress and to provide sentences to let go of the bound energy that causes us to react. We may respond better to following the outlined steps rather than allowing our busy monkey minds to rest unguided for an hour. As with any personal development work, it is beneficial to recruit support and learn through sharing experiences with others. Find friends who have an interest in working with this tool and arrange a workshop or basic training course at your workplace or in your community. Start the conversation on Logosynthesis to help others become comfortable with the topic. You have to experience it to appreciate the beauty.

I Need Someone to Tell Me What to Say

The key to Logosynthesis is the expression of your individual sensations. This is about you and not anyone else. The words and sentences need to express what you are feeling, sensing, and perceiving. They do not express what you think you *should* be feeling nor are they another person's assessment of what is triggering your stress. What has been emotionally imprinted in your personal space is very specific to you. Two people could be at the same event and have completely different emotional imprints, which would trigger very different behaviors. It is also crucial to remember that although it may sound silly, stupid, or irrational when you think about the imprint, emotions don't choose. Acknowledge the sensory perceptions that arise. Apply the three sentences to this imprint. It can be very beneficial to have someone ask questions and guide the process, but it is important that they use your words to describe the imprint. They are not there to fix your problems or offer advice, but to guide the process.

What Is My Life Going to Look Like Now?

An important part of Logosynthesis is determining how to move forward after you have dissolved the imprints that drive your reactions. These habitual patterns have formed your personality and character. Even if you have made only moderate changes, this work can affect your relationships, work, and lifestyle. For me, I trust that if I stay connected to my spiritual energy and Essence, my efforts will be positive for me and for those around me. My life is a journey, and I do not have all the answers, but it feels better to me now. I have let go of things with the trust that I will continue to focus on what is important in my life's purpose so that I can enjoy it more fully.

Chapter 7: Tips for Applying Logosynthesis

We may not feel as though we have time for something new, but we can notice an interesting shift as we begin to create space for the things that are important to us.

Personal Development Is a Process

I have been committed to personal development throughout my career, and I have consumed a lot of expert information along the way. Working in the field of changing consumer attitudes and behaviors throughout my professional career has helped me appreciate the challenges of adopting new habits for wellness. With this background, I am convinced that Logosynthesis is a unique approach to care for self and to appreciate others so that we can enjoy life more fully and better cope with life's challenges. The technique is simple, but it requires repeated practice to be most effective. The philosophy is elegant, but it requires letting go of some beliefs that influence our thinking. To facilitate the learning, I have developed the following tips to reinforce understanding.

Tip 1: Create Space for Your Spirit

There are currently many resources and programs available to care for your body and mind. If you run into trouble, you can access the pharmacy, the doctor's office, or the hospital for a plethora of remedies. Spiritual health doesn't hold the same space in our health care system. Talk of spirit tends to be mainly relegated to religious organizations, but yoga, meditation, art, and individual prayer can also help connect with our spirit.

The goal of Logosynthesis is to restore the flow of Essence or life energy through a guided process. As we release the bound or frozen energy of past events and restore the flow of our Essence, we will not only enhance our spiritual health, but also strengthen our whole being. To incorporate this tool into your life, you need to recognize the importance of spiritual health.

Tip 2: Make Time for Quiet

Logosynthesis requires a quiet, relaxed state. You may find it difficult to find an appropriate time and place. In some cases, even if you carve out a spot, it may be difficult to quiet your mind. Quiet is important for identifying feelings and noticing sensory perceptions. This work involves subtle energy shifts which are difficult to sense if you are preoccupied. Especially as you begin to explore this technique, it is important to recognize that the brain has been conditioned to think, analyze, and explain. Your natural tendency is to avoid negative or uncomfortable feelings, convince yourself that things aren't so bad, and rationalize your coping mechanisms. If you are not familiar with energy work such as Reiki, it may be even more difficult to notice energy shifts. The mind needs to relax from thinking about tasks to be perceptive to energy. I know because this has been a challenge for me.

It can be hard to find time if every hour of every day is planned and accounted for, rushing from one activity or commitment to the next. You are probably convinced that everything you do is important—or if not important, at least entertaining. When you slow down to notice your feelings, you may experience uncomfortable sensations. If so, this may be a good place to start with Logosynthesis. Notice what you are feeling. Allow yourself to experience it, and rate the level of stress. Become aware of your chatter. Identify the sensory perceptions, and apply the sentences. Perhaps you can start to let go of a need to always keep busy and active. Don't force things. Just be aware and willing to try something a little different.

You may have a favorite way to relax. I don't mean with thoughtless activity, such as watching television, chatting on the phone, or scrolling through Facebook. Perhaps there is a quiet place, surrounded by nature, where you can sit quietly. Maybe you can roll out of bed earlier than everyone else in the morning and enjoy alone time. Taking a break by going to an empty meeting room while at work may be beneficial. Make time for some quiet.

I have changed my routines to allow quiet time. I get up earlier to have an hour or two on my own before the bustle of the day begins. I may seek out a beautiful park or a cozy coffee shop on my own while the girls are at a sports practice. When plans change unexpectedly, I take the opportunity to enjoy the moment rather than stress about what I have to do. I have been able to find lots of pockets of unscheduled quiet time and still feel as though I am achieving my goals and enjoying things that are important to me. In fact, I feel less rushed and more productive. Yes, that is a subjective assessment—many people would still classify my life as busy, but I feel like I am in a better spot!

Tip 3: Learn, Train, and Understand the Process

As with any new program, it takes practice to learn the process and time to develop the habit. I personally find it fascinating to know that I can get in touch with triggers that are influencing my stress levels, and simply through the use of three specific sentences, I can release the trigger to reduce my stress. I may have read this during my first introduction to the topic, but I certainly didn't appreciate what it truly meant. Even now, after three years of exploring and applying this work, I know there is much more to learn on the topic. Be patient, persistent, and curious because the results can be intriguing and profound. *Self-Coaching with Logosynthesis: How the Power of Words Can Change Your Life* (Lammers, 2015) is an excellent resource. Try it. Observe. Talk to others.

Of course, as with any learning, a guide or teacher can help enhance our understanding. Logosynthesis is a unique technique within the fields of energy psychology and spirituality. It is still a new technique, however, and the language is still being fine-tuned. The Logosynthesis website will direct you to available resources, which include books, videos and a list of certified practitioners.

We can all learn about Logosynthesis on our own, but significant benefit can be realized from working together.

Tip 4: The Importance of Repetition

Logosynthesis is a technique for guided change that can be incorporated in your daily life. The same technique is repeated over and over again to release energy bound in painful memories and limiting beliefs. As your life progresses, however, events will continue to occur that will cause you to stress. You are not able to control all these events, but the emotional imprints will influence your behavior, personality, and character. Therefore, repeating the Logosynthesis process and engraining it into our routines can be a powerful tool to help deal with what bothers us. The more we use the technique, the easier it is to cope with stress as it arises. Through repetition, we are better able to access the process when we need it the most.

Tip 5: Follow Your Own Path

Around 1990, as president of the Nova Scotia Chapter of the Canadian Celiac Association, I spoke to a group of family physicians about celiac disease and the gluten-free diet to raise awareness and to aid in the diagnosis of what was then a relatively unheard-of condition. At that time, gastroenterologists were able to readily make a diagnosis, but physicians were not recognizing the variations in symptoms and therefore did not refer their patients to specialists. During the coffee break after my talk, one physician informed me that from his professional experience, the recent increase in celiac diagnosis was just a fad and the actual incidence was extremely rare. I perceived his authoritative tone as arrogant and condescending, but doctors were the authority on medical conditions. I questioned whether I should stop speaking on the topic. However, I persisted in my awareness efforts. Thankfully, many others worked relentlessly to tell their stories. Today, the chances of being sick for twenty years prior to diagnosis with celiac disease are significantly lower.

I share this story because it relates to my experience of talking about Logosynthesis. Often, the mention of energy work elicits a look from others that makes me withdraw from further discussion. It's true that I don't have all the answers and can't explain exactly how the technique works. Sometimes, it is extremely easy to believe that others mock or doubt my efforts. But the topic is important, and we have much to learn. Sharing stories and following our own path is important, regardless of what others think. I have used Logosynthesis on these limiting feelings, and I do have confidence and resolve that this material is important and can benefit humanity. People who are familiar with the work share a similar resolve.

Tip 6: Share Your Experiences

I am forthright and outgoing, but my preference is to keep my personal life private. I do not easily share my personal stories, whether accomplishments or struggles. I cope by expressing pleasure when things go well, expressing frustration when things don't go my way, and keeping things that are personal and important to me to myself.

An extremely interesting observation for me is that the more I use Logosynthesis to dissolve my triggers and neutralize my reactions, the less attached I am to my emotions. Situations from my past that I was never comfortable sharing with anyone no longer have the same stronghold on me. When I realize that I am reacting to something from my past and I have a tool to release the energy in the trigger, I feel a great sense of freedom.

I have learned that it is important to share my personal experiences with Logosynthesis so that others may benefit. We all have experiences from our pasts that continue to cause us stress in the here and now.

Often, we believe our reactions are unique; however, we all react through a similar process. The more we can appreciate that these reactions are normal (although the severity may vary based on the intensity of the initial event) and that they can be deactivated through a tested technique, the more we can begin to create a space for others to do their own work.

Tip 7: Appreciate with Patience and Grace

You may wish to experiment with other forms of energy work and meditation to help you get in touch with energy sensations and move to more positive energy vibrations. For me, Logosynthesis has allowed for a very unique and targeted approach to help reduce my stress and connect with my energy. Given my results-oriented, goal-focused approach to life, this method works for me.

But I have learned that transformation does not happen overnight. If you are dealing with the stress of a traumatic event, you may notice a significant release after applying the sentences to the emotional imprint. For less traumatic events, you may notice a more subtle release of frozen energy. Have confidence that the process works. Have the persistence to continue to explore various areas of your stress, identify your triggers, and release your frozen energy. These emotional imprints can be complex in nature and may not resolve with one session. There is more than one imprint in your personal space. Be comfortable knowing that everything doesn't need to be resolved at once. Unless it is causing you or those around you stress, it may not need to be resolved at all. Don't overthink it. Be patient. It is part of the journey.

Tip 8: You Don't Need to Change Everything

The premise of Logosynthesis is that the Self, our Essence, does not suffer. As life happens, our reaction to events creates emotional imprints that are frozen in our personal space and block the flow of life energy. If we can allow ourselves to recognize how we suffer, rather than suppressing our suffering, we can begin to identify the sensory perceptions that have imprinted in our personal space. Using the power of words to direct our energy to dissolve the imprints allows us to free the flow of energy and remove the triggers to our stress and habitual patterns of behavior. Over the course of our life, we have experienced a large number of events, some more traumatic and strongly imprinted than others. Some result in more stress and suffering than others.

As we begin to work with Logosynthesis, we can identify which situations we want to prioritize. Of course, my approach to life would entail picking the big items right away, solving them, and moving on. However, Logosynthesis is a gentle approach. Applying the sentences requires feeling safe and being receptive to the process. The key part of the exercise is becoming aware of how you experience your stress and being open to exploring what lies underneath the surface.

Logosynthesis does not require that you rehash your past, but that you become aware of what currently bothers you and identify the sensory perceptions. These are often sights, sounds, and even smells from your past. Three key areas that cause suffering are painful memories, fear of the future, and limiting beliefs. It may be beneficial to start working with mild suffering to become comfortable with the process.

Each of us is unique, and this diversity makes our world an interesting place. We don't have to change everything about ourselves. However, given that chronic stress negatively impacts health and creates stress in those around us, it is important work. Once you can acknowledge that things do bother you, and are willing to change it, you can start your journey through Logosynthesis.

Chapter 8: Enjoying Life with Logosynthesis

We are all unique. We all have an opportunity to enhance our current life experience by addressing our unique triggers to stress. Be supportive of the efforts of others.

Our Personal Goals

We can all benefit from enjoying life more fully. We can all benefit from letting go of the energy bound in our limiting beliefs, our painful memories, and our pre-conceived notions of the way that life should be. As we begin to neutralize our reactions, we can create space for things that are important in our life. Rather than constantly reacting to the urgent demands that arise, we can begin to focus our energy on our life purpose. We can begin to achieve our personal goals within the framework of the life we currently live.

Over the years, I have devoted considerable effort to personal development and changing my behaviors. Based on all my learning, I am convinced that we cannot get to the level of stress reduction and behavior change that we need to see in our society through cognitive thinking alone. We need to access our energy and our spirit.

We may be proud of our health initiatives with their measurable interventions, but there is something less visible affecting our beliefs and behaviors. We need to acknowledge our spiritual being and the power of our energy, both personally and as a society. Society tells us how life should be, and we react to the fact that our life is not that way. We can feel tremendous pressure to live up to the expectations that we feel from society - the messages we receive through conversations and the media; from peers and experts. And our reactions may not be beneficial.

It may be easy to discount the work outlined in this book because I have not provided objective, measurable, and repeatable proof that we require to validate all our scientific assumptions. Given my experience, I have come to realize that I don't have to wait for all the data to be in and the authorities to tell me that it is valid. I am confident that this philosophy and technique can have significant impact. And we can start now. I challenge each and every one of us to be open to the potential of this work. We can then discover ways to work together to better measure the results.

I challenge each and every one of us to begin to incorporate this process into our lives. Students and teachers. Children and parents. Employees and bosses. Citizens and leaders. It is important to take time to recognize our feelings and beliefs, to be aware of our sensory perceptions, and to allow the power of the Logosynthesis sentences to allow frozen energy to shift. There may be a lot of triggers. No worries. We can start wherever we are.

I also challenge us to not discount the efforts of others. It is worthwhile to apply the process to our reactions about the validity of this work to create space to explore. This work is personal. With practice, we will get more comfortable with the process and recognize the value for ourselves and for others.

I challenge that we look for opportunity to apply Logosynthesis not only in our personal lives, but also in our communities. Many people who can truly benefit from Logosynthesis are not currently in a position to access it.

For many, life is overwhelming, and they do not have the available energy to start the process. We need to create space for them to feel safe. This is not a complicated tool, but we require an environment that supports it.

My personal goal is to let go of my reactions so that I can live and enjoy my life in the present. This is not something that has come easily to me in the past. However, as I work with Logosynthesis, I feel that I can finally neutralize my reactions and let go of my need to control things. I am experiencing a very noticeable shift in how I experience life.

I'm okay walking through my house when it is messy rather than tensing up because things are out of place.

I'm okay trying to explain things to someone who should already understand them.

I'm okay expressing my ideas without worrying that someone might think I'm a little out there.

I'm okay recognizing that I can't fix everything around me and that I don't need to control it all.

I'm okay acknowledging that I still have work to do.

These are small shifts that I am sure most people would not even notice. For me, there is a subtle, but dramatic difference in how my body feels every day. It's not a "so what" attitude. It's more of a "that's okay" attitude. And for me, I now feel that I'm okay, even when things don't go my way.

Self-Care and Caring for Others

We all develop coping mechanisms to deal with the stress of our environment. We can become very efficient at self-regulating so that the external demands placed on us do not exceed our resources. This may come at an expense to those close to us. A boss may delegate excessive work on subordinates. Parents may prioritize work demands over their children's needs. Teachers may avoid feeling overwhelmed with demands of work and home by limiting their involvement with students. We cope, but we have an opportunity to do better for society.

For many of us, we are concerned about the well-being of those who are close to us. We want to fix their problems and take away their pain. Our energy is directed to those who are more vulnerable with the recognition that we will get by. A local politician was struck by the number of veterans who approached his office looking for support not for themselves, but for peers who were suffering. Despite significant issues of their own, their focus was to help remove the pain and suffering of others. At times, we can neglect our needs to support the needs of others.

Much of the initial development of Logosynthesis has focused on self-care for individuals working in the healing professions. If we can begin to let go of the energy we hold in our beliefs about what life should look like for others, we can create the space for them to better explore their reactions to their limiting beliefs, their painful memories, and their notions about how life should be. As we begin to let go of things that are not important and neutralize our reactions, people will begin to notice a shift in our tone and energy. We will have our energy more available to support others so they can build their resources to enjoy life more fully.

Living Life Now

I'm not sure I am doing it all right.

Actually, I am sure I am not doing it all right.

Although I've taken courses and consulted Logosynthesis practitioners, I know that I could get even better results with more focus.

I am busy living my life. I focus on my work. I am the mother of two active girls and the wife of a successful small business owner. I enjoy getting together with friends. I don't have a great deal of time to spend on this, but I feel quite comfortable with my progress.

I don't experience anxiety nor am I dealing with a trauma. I don't think I am inflicting a crazy amount of stress on others, but I continue to encounter things that sidetrack me. I react to situations with frustration, and I feel stress. Now, however, I am aware that my stress is telling me something. When I find myself reacting inappropriately, I simply make a note to take some time to apply Logosynthesis. It might be that evening or the next morning. It may even be the next week or the next month, but I hold in my awareness that my response has been activated by something in my past. I am aware that I am reacting, and I usually take the initiative to work on it.

I have made more progress in reducing my stress and changing my habitual behaviors in the past year than I have in the past forty years. Therefore, I am confident that I am doing something right. People may dismiss me or downplay my results, but I don't mind.

In exploring Logosynthesis, I have learned that when life happens around me, I have habitually reacted to make myself feel better. I have responded based on my fantasies of how things should be. My unique past experiences trigger my behavior to change things to align with my beliefs. But as I release these triggers, I don't have to react. When my energy is aligned to Essence, I can take thoughtful action rather than reacting under habitual distress.

Maybe it is all in my head. There are no textbooks that can scientifically explain the cause-effect I have experienced with Logosynthesis. Not yet. However, based on my personal and professional experience, I am confident that this process works. I'm not certain what will transpire down the road, but that's okay. I have discovered a beautiful, graceful way of letting go of beliefs that have controlled my behavior for a very long time, beliefs that no longer serve me well and cause me to react inappropriately. It requires nothing except trust in the process and the ability to sit quietly to get in touch with my emotions and sensory perceptions, followed by three sentences and pauses to allow the words to process.

You can start now with nothing more than this book to guide you to take the first step in creating space to enjoy life more fully and live your life with purpose.

Amazing!

Suggested Reading

The following is a list of books that I have enjoyed and that have provided me with material to ponder and explore. While I have heard many comments about my choice of reading material, I find all of these books intriguing. In some cases, one author led me to another. At other times, I simply read what was available to download from the library. Others books caught my eye in a store or at the airport. I suggest that you develop your own reading list and approach a broad range of resources with an open and inquiring mind to see where they lead you. It is my desire that this book is included in your list of suggested reading for expanding thinking and broadening perspectives. Enjoy!

Brzezinski, Mika. Knowing Your Value: Women, Money, and Getting What You're Worth. New York: Weinstein, 2011.

Bstan-'dzin-rgya-mtsho. The Universe in a Single Atom: The Convergence of Science and Spirituality. New York: Morgan Road, 2005.

Chopra, Deepak and Tanzi, Rudolph E. Super Brain: Unleashing the Explosive Power of Your Mind to Maximize Health, Happiness, and Spiritual Well-being. Harmony, 2013.

Chopra, Deepak. God: A Story of Revelation. New York: HarperOne, 2012.

DiSalvo, David. What Makes Your Brain Happy and Why You Should Do the Opposite. Amherst, NY: Prometheus, 2011.

Dispenza, Joe. Breaking the Habit of Being Yourself: How to Lose Your Mind and Create a New One. Carlsbad, CA: Hay House, 2012.

Dispenza, Joe. You Are the Placebo: Making Your Mind Matter. Hay House, 2014.

Duhigg, Charles. The Power of Habit: Why We Do What We Do in Life and Business. New York: Random House, 2012.

Dyer, Wayne W. Excuses Begone!: How to Change Lifelong, Self-defeating Thinking Habits. Carlsbad, CA: Hay House, 2009.

Dyer, Wayne W. Manifest Your Destiny: The Nine Spiritual Principles for Getting Everything You Want. New York: HarperCollins, 1997.

Dyer, Wayne W. The Shift: Taking Your Life from Ambition to Meaning. Carlsbad, CA: Hay House, 2010.

Gladwell, Malcolm. Blink: The Power of Thinking Without Thinking. New York: Little, Brown, 2005.

Gladwell, Malcolm. What the Dog Saw: And Other Adventures. London: Penguin, 2010.

Goleman, Daniel. Emotional Intelligence. New York: Bantam, 1996.

Goleman, Daniel. Social Intelligence: The New Science of Human Relationships. New York: Bantam, 2006.

Grant, Adam M. Give and Take: A Revolutionary Approach to Success. New York, NY: Viking, 2013.

Hawking, Stephen, and Mlodinow, Leonard. A Briefer History of Time. New York: Bantam, 2005.

Hawkins, David R. Power vs. Force: The Hidden Determinants of Human Behavior. Carlsbad, CA: Hay House, 2002.

Hay, Louise L, and Tomchin, Linda Carwin. The Power Is Within You. Carson, CA: Hay House, 1991.

Hay, Louise L., and Susan Gross. Heal Your Body A–Z: The Mental Causes for Physical Illness and the Way to Overcome Them. Carlsbad (California): Hay House, 2009.

Hicks, Esther, Hicks, Jerry, and Abraham. The Vortex: Where the Law of Attraction Assembles All Cooperative Relationships. Carlsbad, CA: Hay House, 2009.

Hillenbrand, Laura. Unbroken: A World War II Story of Survival, Resilience, and Redemption. New York: Random House, 2010.

Huffington, Arianna Stassinopoulos. Thrive: The Third Metric to Redefining Success and Creating a Happier Life. London: WH Allen, 2014.

Lammers, Willem. Self-coaching with Logosynthesis: How the Power of Words Can Change Your Life. Maienfeld: CreateSpace, 2015.

Lammers, Willem. Logosynthesis: Healing with Words. Maienfeld: CreateSpace, 2015.

Losier, Michael J. Law of Attraction. London: Hodder Mobius, 2008.

Manz, Charles C. The Power of Failure: 27 Ways to Turn Life's Setbacks into Success. San Francisco: Berrett-Koehler, 2002.

Maté, Gabor. When the Body Says No: Understanding the Stress-Disease Connection. Hoboken, NJ: J. Wiley, 2003.

Mindell, Phyllis. How to Say It for Women: Communicating with Confidence and Power Using the Language of Success. Paramus: Prentice Hall, 2001.

Nakazawa, Donna Jackson. Childhood Disrupted: How Your Biography Becomes Your Biology, and How You Can Heal. Atria Books, 2015.

Neffinger, John and Kohut, Matthew. Compelling People: The Hidden Qualities That Make Us Influential. Hudson Street Press, 2013.

Pink, Daniel H. Drive: The Surprising Truth about What Motivates Us. New York: Riverhead, 2009.

Pink, Daniel H. A Whole New Mind: Why Right-brainers Will Rule the Future. New York: Riverhead, 2006.

Read, Piers Paul. Alive: The Story of the Andes Survivors. Philadelphia: Lippincott, 1974.

Schwartz, Barry, and Sharpe, Kenneth. Practical Wisdom: The Right Way to Do the Right Thing. New York: Riverhead, 2010.

Susanka, Sarah. The Not So Big Life: Making Room for What Really Matters. New York: Random House, 2007.

Tolle, Eckhart. A New Earth: Awakening to Your Life's Purpose. New York: Plume, 2006.

Tolle, Eckhart. The Power of Now: A Guide to Spiritual Enlightenment. Novato, CA: New World Library, 1999.

Turok, Neil. The Universe Within: From Quantum to Cosmos. Crows Nest, NSW: Allen & Unwin, 2013.

Vedantam, Shankar. The Hidden Brain: How Our Unconscious Minds Elect Presidents, Control Markets, Wage Wars, and Save Our Lives. New York: Spiegel & Grau, 2010.

Weiss, Dr. Laurie. Letting It Go. Relieve Anxiety and Toxic Stress in Just a Few Minutes Using Only Words. Littleton, CO: Empowerment Systems Books, 2016.

Printed in the USA
CPSIA information can be obtained
at www.ICGtesting.com
LVHW090848131023
760813LV00031B/1282/J